DAYLIGHT INFLUENCE ON COLOUR DESIGN

Author: Maud Hårleman

Title: Daylight Influence on Colour Design

Empirical study on Perceived Colour and Colour Experience Indoors

PhD Dissertation/Akademisk avhandling 2007

KTH, School of Architecture and the Built Environment
School of Architecture
Royal Institute of Technology
SE-100 44 Stockholm
Sweden

TRITA-ARK-Akademisk avhandling 2007:3
ISSN 1402-7461
ISRN KTH/ARK/AA—07:03—SE
ISBN (KTH) 978-91-7178-667-8
Revised Edition

Printed by Printfinder, Riga 2007

Axl Books, Stockholm 2007
www.axlbooks.com
info@axlbooks.com

ISBN 978-91-976644-0-0

DAYLIGHT INFLUENCE ON COLOUR DESIGN

EMPIRICAL STUDY ON PERCEIVED COLOUR AND COLOUR EXPERIENCE INDOORS

MAUD HÅRLEMAN

ABSTRACT

It is known that one and the same interior colouring will appear different in rooms with windows facing north or facing south, but it is not known how natural daylight from these two compass points affects perceived colour and the ways in which colour is experienced. The objective is to describe the perceived colours to be expected in rooms with sunlight and diffused light, and thus develop a tool for colour design. *Two empirical investigations* provide the basis for six attached papers. The model is exploratory with a qualitative character. One hundred and ninety-one studies were carried out with 79 observers in full-scale rooms, with double-glazed transparent room windows facing north or south. The NCS colour sample collection and colour terminology were used, with three yellow, red, blue and green hues in two nuances: whitish 1010 and more chromatic 1030. The walls were painted in a total of 23 selected inherent colours with each colour observed in up to 10 studies. *Colour matching* was achieved using a *colour reference box* and results were analysed with the aid of the terms *inherent colour* and *identity colour*. The colour reference box was tested in a separate study to investigate any methodological problems. Room character was described using *semantic differentials*, and data was processed using the SPSS *statistics program*. *Verbal description using own words* was applied in a *descriptive and reflecting method* to find sensory differences and precise, yet ordinary descriptions. Colour differences between rooms were assessed using verbal description of hue and nuance, and a supplementary method with *specified colour samples*. *Emotional impressions* of colour and rooms were assessed using a *method describing primary emotions* and the results were compared with results from another study using small colour samples. The *colouring* that enhanced or neutralised room light situation was compared as regards emotional impression and thereafter compared with results from another study.

Daylight from the different compass points caused a clear shift in hue and nuance. The perceived colour was consistently more chromatic and less whitish than the inherent colour used. Nuance 1010 shifted more in hue, while 1030 instead increased most in chromaticness. Even minor colour differences resulted in major differences in colour experience.

The north-facing room in yellowish colours shifted towards reduced yellowishness in both hue and chromaticness. Indications were that north-facing rooms in reddish blue become more reddish than south-facing rooms.

Key words: *architecture; interior colouring; spatial character; natural daylight; verbal description; colour reference box.*

CONTENTS

LIST OF ATTACHED PAPERS

Paper 1: Hårleman, M; Colour Appearance in Different Compass Orientations. Published in *Nordic Architectural Research* 2, 2001.

Paper 2: Billger, M & Hårleman, M; A Method for Comparison of Colour Appearance in Differently Illuminated Rooms. Published in CIE´s conference proceedings, publication 133, vol. 1. part. 67-71, 1999. My input consists of method tests, contribution with own empirical results and shared responsibility for text.

Paper 3: Hårleman, M; Study of Colour Shifts in Various Daylights. Dominantly reddish and greenish colours in different compass orientations. A comparative study of colour shift in rooms illuminated with different qualities of daylight. Submitted to *Colour: Design and Creativity* May 31, 2006, accepted for publication Jan 10, 2007. www.sdc.org.uk.

Paper 4: Hårleman, M, Werner, I-B, Billger, M; Significance of Colour on Spatial Character. Study on north and south facing rooms in dominantly reddish and greenish inherent colours. Submitted to *Colour: Design and Creativi*ty Feb 2, 2007, accepted for publication June 4, 2007. A shorter version published in *Design & Emotions* 2006 in Göteborg, no. 154 in proceedings on CD. My input consists of planning and implementation of study and main responsibility for text.

Paper 5: Hårleman, M; Colour Emotion in Full- scale Rooms. Published in AIC (Association International de la Couleur) proceedings 2004, pp. 223-226.

Paper 6: Stahre, B, Hårleman, M. and Billger, M; Colour Emotions in Larger and Smaller Scale. Published in AIC proceedings 2004, pp. 27-30. My input consists of analysis of comparative data, discussion of results and shared responsibility for text.

All papers peer reviewed.

PREFACE

Colours and their effect have always been of great interest to me and colour has been a natural ingredient in everything I've done. Like all other doctoral students I at first thought I would be able to investigate many more aspects offered by the subject. When I now finally attach six papers, all dealing with at least one aspect, I still feel a sense of satisfaction. My wish now is simply that my work will come to use and that it will be easier for architects and designers to reach predetermined results with a colouring design. After all, this is where my heart is: in consideration of good environments giving a sense of well-being and stimulation; in a firm conviction as to the importance of design; and not least in a love of colour as phenomenon and perpetual source of pleasure to many people.

When attending interior designer studies at the University College of Arts, Crafts and Design in Stockholm, we tested light cabinets with varying types of artificial illumination to gain an understanding of the relations between light and colour. The cabinets contained incandescent and fluorescent lights with various colour rendering indices, and we switched lights on and off and compared visual perceptions from colour samples we inserted. It taught us the importance of control over lighting to be used if colouring is to be right. We also learnt that daylight from different compass points makes colour and spatial quality appear different despite identical colouring. Previous classes had done practical work on studies of light and colour, but no assembled material existed from this work and there was no presentation of findings. It was silent knowledge, private and unworded. This was something that gnawed at me in my professional life, something I determined to put right. It was also important to investigate the nature of colour beyond colour code: colour effect and how colour and space are experienced. It is frequently stated in articles and reports: Use cool blue hues in sunny rooms. Use sun-yellow to add warmth to dark, cool rooms. How does this work? Can colours provide warmth and cool? And what is the nature of colour impressions, now there is a chance to take a closer look?

My foremost thanks go to my supervisor Professor Jadwiga Krupinska at the Royal Institute of Technology (KTH) in Stockholm and associate supervisor Docent Monica Billger at Chalmers University of Technology in Göteborg. Without your unwavering help and support this thesis would not have come to fruition. Also special thanks to assistant supervisor Docent Inga-Britt Werner at KTH who has been invaluable in giving knowledgeable support and is co-author of the section with statistical calculations. Thanks to Jan Janssens, researcher at Lunds Technical University, LTH, for being opponent on my closing seminar, Dr Cecilia Häggström LTH and Prof. Armand Björkman senior lecturer at Chalmers for taking on at my licentiate seminar. Thanks to Dr Karin Fridell Anter, Professor Anders Liljefors, KTH, my former assistant supervisor Björner Torsson, KTH, Prof. Ulf Keijer, KTH, and Prof. Hans Allan Löfberg at Statens Institut för Byggnadsforskning, for valuable help and interest. Not to forget Docent Magnus Rönn and Docent Abdellah Abarkan at KTH. My friends and colleagues as Phd students have of course been highly important both in criticism and encouragement: Eva Bergdahl, Kerstin Lyckman, Åsa Dahlin, Inger Norell, Catharina Nord, Katrin Fagerström, Marie Ferring, Gertrud Olsson, Monica Sand and others. I would also like to thank architect and artist Anders Berglund who helped with the initial full-scale studies. How fortunate you all exist!

Many thanks to the following for financial backing: *Formas* (Swedish Research Council for Environment, Agricultural Sciences and Spatial Planning with first Stefan Stridh and later on Margareta Björnberg as contact persons; *Måleriutveckling*, an organisation made up of the Swedish painters' union - with Lars-Åke Lundin - and *Målaremästarna* (trade and employers association of Swedish painting contractors) - with Diana Uppman. Without your genuine interest and generous contributions this project would not have been achieved. Thanks to the foundation Lars Hiertas minne and Ulla Johansson at *Alcro-Beckers* who provided all the paint required. The Scandinavian Colour Institute contributed with electronic software. Staffan at Axl Books has been a blessing in making a book out of my manuscript with lots of humour (and coffey). Finally I would of course like to thank my loving and patient family for support and encouragement. Thank you Vera for your kind and financial support. To Christian, Mimmi, Kalle and Lasse, there is only one thing to say: a new era is now approaching!

INTRODUCTION

1. PRESENTATION

> Why is the sky blue? – Because radiated white light from the sun spreads into the atmosphere on its way to us, mainly due to small density variations in the air space, but also due to atmospheric contaminants of various kinds. Above all, this affects the short-wave radiation that is disseminated and provides the sky with its blue colour. At the same time the direct sunlight loses part of this radiation and gains a yellowish complimentary colour hue. J. Sisefsky, 1995, p. 128

Colour is a design tool that provides colour characteristics and expressions in design. A planned colouring should provide the expected result. Failure here is an irritation. With public premises or other larger buildings it is sometimes costly or time-wise practically impossible to re-paint. Having control over results so that selected colouring has the desired effect is thus of double importance. The problem is that light and colour are so intimately entwined: all lighting affects the colour we will see. Various types of artificial lighting such as incandescent, fluorescent, halogen etc cause differences in colour, just as various types of daylight do. Identical colouring will appear different in rooms with sunlight and rooms with diffused sky light, and hence also in rooms facing various points on the compass. This difficulty is well known, but no systematic studies have been made of the relations.

> Imagine walking along a corridor in an office block. It is morning, the sun is shining, and as we walk we glimpse through the open doors of the various rooms on each side of the corridor. We immediately notice that the walls in the rooms are differently coloured: on one side they are pale light pink and on the other a sharper bluish pink. We assume, however, that the architect

> gave them the same colour and sees it as a failure when despite intentions they appear different. Or else, perhaps we see the colour variation as an advantage, telling us as it does of the sun's journey and compass orientation of the rooms. Alternatively, we might have preferred the architect to have avoided this and instead used different colours on each side of the corridor.
> M. Hårleman, 2000

My interest in these issues arose from practical experiences working as an interior designer. The colour difference resulting from light relations in different rooms was greater than I expected. I began looking for a method for dealing with this. My primary interest was in knowing how to predict and calculate colour differences. I also wished to encounter an experience-based way of relating to this – how do aware practitioners deal with these issues? I could find no method of predicting the colour differences that would arise, but on the other hand I found many opinions as to how the problem should be dealt with. Most people nowadays appear to aim at neutralising the differences between rooms with "warm" and "cool" light, i.e. south and north-facing rooms. The recommendation prior to this was however an intensification of the light situation with the aid of room colouring. One such advocate of this was the renowned architecture theorist Steen Eiler Rasmussen.

> When we recall such a building we remember it as a composition of many rooms of different character in which daylight and its colours play a decisive role. Instead of trying to make the cool rooms warm it is possible to do just the opposite by employing colors that emphasize their cool atmosphere. Even when the sun is warmest and most brilliant, daylight in northern rooms will have a blue undertone because all light here is, after all, solely and exclusively reflection from the sky. Blue and other cool colors show with great brilliance in northern rooms while warm colors show up poorly, as if seen under a lamp that sheds a bluish light. Therefore, if in northern rooms cool colors are used and in southern rooms warm colors, all of the colors will sparkle in their full radiance.
> S. E. Rasmussen, 1959, p 223.

Rasmussen writes convincingly on the advantages of enhancing colours, but also writes about the *sensory impressions* colours can give us. Colour is not of course simply about *perception* but is just as much about colour experience. Our experience of colour includes the immediate sensory impressions produced by perception. This thesis deals with colour both as perception and experience. The word 'perception' derives from the Latin *percipere* 'seize' 'understand' and *per* 'entirely' *capere* 'take' (OED 1998), and is thus seen as apprehension through which information on one's surroundings is fully taken in. The colour experience also includes connotations, associations and feelings/states of mind. This is why knowledge is also needed of the psychological consequences of colour variations occurring in rooms.

1.1 Disposition

The thesis is based on two empirical investigations. In their turn these resulted in six papers based on part-studies. These are preceded by a presentation in seven chapters where the project is set forth and its most important component parts are summarised.

1. The first chapter describes how work was initiated and the project set up. This features points of departure and questions, as well as a brief presentation of development of the project through the two phases.
2. The first section of this chapter deals with terminology used. The theoretical background of the subject follows this. The relation between light radiation energy and the colour we see is complicated, and here are presented physical and psychological aspects affecting colour vision and colour experience. A description of current research on colour phenomena is given with particular regard to colours spatial effects.
3. In the third chapter the project methods are described: both those common to the two investigations and the development of methods prior to these. The first empirical investigation resulted in a licentiate thesis after which the questions at issue were given both new width and depth.
4. Some of the most important observations and methods are discussed in chapter four. Also discussed are the way in which the project performed and the way in which the various studies relate to one another.

5. Conclusions as regards the entire project are summarised in chapter five. New issues are raised on the basis of the knowledge gained and experiences arising from the project.

6-7. Lists of reference and other literature follow this. Then finally the appendices: two questionnaires plus figures and tables. Those who wish to look further into the various studies and methods of the project are referred to each respective paper as given in the table of contents. Each individual study is expanded on in the papers. It may otherwise suffice to read introductory and summary chapters.

1.2 Beginnings

The point of departure for the project was the variations of natural daylight to be found in Sweden, and the differences in light quality in north and south-facing rooms that represent different prerequisites in relation to colour and design. This entails identical paint colours used in north and south-facing rooms appearing different.

> The structure of light at the equator is horizontal, with a rhythm of 12 hrs.
> At the North Pole it is vertical, with a rhythm of six months.
> Vesa Honkonen 2003 [1]

A further point of departure was the use of all four chromatic elementary colours (yellow, red, blue, green) in nuances that may be seen in internal colouring. The third point of departure was that colours would be studied in their context, i.e. in full-scale rooms with natural daylight. What then characterises our natural daylight in Scandinavia, what are the preconditions?

> In a south-facing room we make contact with the living, the variability of weather, the shifting intensity of sunlight; changes in a room when sunlight falls on delightful spheres from specks of dust floating in otherwise unseen movements.

1. A Finnish architect, well known for his work with urban lighting, presented himself and his interest for light in G. Wessel's research project on light and colour.

> The warm colours from sunlight fills the entire room, and the rays of sunlight feel their way like giant fingers over the tabletop, down to the floor and further into the room. Ascending the walls they create patterns that turn as time fly.
> M. Hårleman, 2000 p.11

> When I then venture into a north-facing room, I can feel over my entire body how my skin cools. It is like going from sun into a shadow. Being in shadow is restful – no longer to be observed. The light in a northern room is relatively constant; you are not instantly aware of how the sun is moving across the heavens, becoming aware only at dawn and dusk or when a change in weather takes place. Such changes hint the existence of time. This economy is soothing.
> M. Hårleman, 2000 p. 11

Identical colourings in rooms facing different compass points will appear different. This is due to light conditions prevailing in the Scandinavian countries in particular and to some degree in the British Isles. Latitude, season, angle of sun, climate, humidity level, weather and quality of air are all parameters that influence conditions of light. Countries with a dry and sunny climate have stable weather systems where sunny weather and a constant intensity of illumination can be counted on, making it relatively simple to calculate level of light when planning buildings (Hopkinson et al 1966, p 17). In the southern hemisphere the sun stands higher in the sky, the result being rooms with more similar illumination. In our temperate climate weather changes rapidly and frequently, and calculating intensity of illumination in buildings is much more difficult. Cloud cover means lower levels of illumination and few hours of sunshine, in which case there is no difference in north and south-facing rooms, but the variations are very wide between different situations. Differences between north and south-facing rooms dealt with in this thesis largely occur in the northern hemisphere. The latitudes of Scandinavia are approximately 57-75° together with southern Greenland, northern Canada and Siberia, meaning the sun is low in its trajectory and light falls at a slant, resulting in low intensity of illumination. Stockholm is at 60° latitude. A higher intensity of illumination can sometimes be experienced in winter when the air is dry and relatively clean and clear. The low trajectory of the sun further results in north and south-facing rooms being reached to a greater degree by light with different characteristics. On clear days south-facing rooms are lit by direct sunlight and reflected sky light, while north-facing rooms are lit by diffused light and indirect sunlight. Spectral distribution and intensity of illumination differ for these light characteristics, giving the rooms different appearances. The relationship between north and south is reversed in the southern hemisphere. (Figure 1 and 2.)

The sum of direct and diffuse solar radiation is entitled global radiation. If the sky is clear or overcast, description of this is relatively simple. But if the sky is partly covered by clouds, then there may be large variations in total heat and light radiation (Löfberg 1976).

The spectral composition of daylight varies considerably and there is no simple formula for calculating it. The colour temperature of daylight varies between 3,800 K and 40,000 K depending on the calculations from different researchers (Löfberg 1976, p 12). (Figure 3.)

Beyond this are other factors influencing the character of incident light: room height and situation in building, relation to vegetation, ground and surface outside, window size and position, colour of window frames, single, double or triple glazing and glass surface treatment if any, along with neighbouring façades and their materials and colours.

1.3 Problems Faced

The thesis deals with internal colouring with a focus on room wall colours. Rooms that surround us make up the environment in which we spend a large part of our lives. Architects, designers, painters and practitioners use colour and colouring to create positive, stimulating and pleasant environments. Colour is one of several design tools. Colouring is often used to produce a specific spatial character to be passed on to users, such as emotional warmth and group solidarity. Perhaps the aim is for collaboration between several different units by holding them together against others with help from colour. In which case architects need to know results in advance, know how a colour sample will appear on four walls and in varying light conditions. The problem is not that rooms illuminated chiefly with sunlight or diffused light will appear differently. The problem is that architects or designers responsible for the colouring have difficulties in knowing the results in advance. This lack of knowledge causes uncertainty that may result in the architects failing in their intentions. Rectifying such mistakes can be very expensive. Frequently this means leaving matters as they are, to the disadvantage of users. The same lack of knowledge is also the basis of colouring where ambition is low and architects are unable to use the full range of colour possibilities. Common concerns are that rooms will feel too cool or warm, too small or large, too hard, dark or drab. As regards warm and cool, these concerns turn up in particular with regard to colouring in north and south-facing rooms.

Traditional colour research has been conducted on two-dimensional colour objects.[2] If the results of research are to be used by architects in practical work then fresh colour studies in three-dimensional environments are required. Spatial area provides a more complicated interplay between simultaneous contrasts and the effects of reflection. In real environments we are surrounded by colour and space and are influenced by a whole spectrum of factors, such as overall impression and spatiality, colour differences between surfaces, light differences and wall texture.

The intention of this project was to join together assessments of perceived colour with descriptions of mental experience of the same colour. I looked for logicality or a broader pattern in investigative material. This gave me the idea to carry out an exploratory investigation with considerable opportunities to encourage observers to use their own descriptions. It was important here to use several different methods to assess perception and experience and then link experience to room characteristics.

1.3.1 Main Issues and Objective

Colour can help change an individual's experience of a room and at the same time be the source of emotional impressions. If knowledge is lacking as to how a specific colour will appear in a room illuminated by natural daylight, then full use of the possibilities made available by colour is difficult. Achieving results as planned becomes a problem. Similarly there is a lack of knowledge as to if and how daylight from vari-

2. See section 2.3 on field of research.

ous compass points and various qualities of light affect experiences of colour and space. This at present represents a hitch, something that each individual including professional architects must learn by experience. Thus development of knowledge on perceived colour and colour experience is essential. The main issues are:

- how do selected inherent colours appear in north and south-facing rooms?
- how are the rooms experienced?
- do different colours result in differing emotional experiences?
- do north and south compass points cause differences in spatial character?

Project objective was to contribute to greater knowledge on and awareness of colour. Thus colour, space and daylight are all treated on the basis of differences in light quality relating to compass point. Groups targeted are researchers, architects and designers, and the goal is that conclusions from the thesis will be applicable to colouring in internal spaces.

1.3.2. Delimitations

The two phases of the project were limited to the latitudes of Stockholm but results – with greater deviations – can be assumed to apply to much larger areas. Assessment of physiological and physical causal relations was limited to background information. Factors other than compass points that contribute to varying appearance of the used colours were not treated. Despite this, a degree of basic knowledge makes it easier to understand how compass direction can possibly cause shifts in *hue* and *nuance*. Terminology used is explained in section 2.1. More in-depth information is available in reference literature.

As far as possible I have attempted to treat immediate experience of colour and space. The symbolic content of colour was not dealt with, nor was colour as semiotic pointer. Though full refinement of questions so as to exclude such aspects is not possible – colour is a complex phenomenon. My standpoint concerning the personal preferences of observers was that there was no wish to investigate them, but neither was it entirely possible to ignore them. The exploratory, reflective method can be equated with interview technique, common in qualitative research. In such a perspective personal experiences and preferences are not to be ignored, but were balanced out here by a relatively large quantity of studies.

1.4 Project Development

The thesis is based on two empirical investigations in full-scale rooms in natural daylight, with a focus on colour in north and south-facing directions. The observations were carried out between 9 am and 3 pm during two Stockholm summers. The investigations were of qualitative character and two chief methods for description and understanding were used: one *method for judging the perceived colour* and one *method for assessing the experience.* Hue shift was described with the help of a colour matching method using a colour reference box. The set of issues was processed from a design perspective using a descriptive, reflective method. Glass panes in the experiment room were not coated nor tinted. Room walls were painted 23 times and assessed by observers with regard to perceived colour and colour experience.

1.4.1 Phase 1, Yellow-Blue Investigation

If we wish to gain greater control over design processes then colour has to be studied in its context – in this case interiors in daylight. One task was to pinpoint how colours selected would vary depending on compass orientation of the room concerned. A further task was to assess how the rooms could appear in a broader sense. This phase was presented in my licentiate thesis (Hårleman 2000).

- How do specific selected inherent colours appear in north and south-facing rooms?
- How do the rooms appear in the colours?
- How might the differences between the rooms be described?

The questions touch upon an interpretation of the situation: how the various room planes – with floor, corners and ceiling - result in reflections and the effects of light being cast back; what identity colours[3] and colour variations appear in the two compass directions. The full-scale studies were conducted in a construction cabin positioned with windows facing either north or south. All four walls were painted successively in yellow and blue inherent colours and assessed with regard to both perceived colour and colour experience. The intention was to describe colour as a

3. See section entitled Colour Concepts.

phenomenon and observer experience of seeing it in the room. There were two perspectives to the issue: a *colour perspective* and a *spatial perspective*, with both affected by differences in hue and nuance. Perceived colour was assessed and related to compass orientation. I used the term *identity colour* as a variation of perceived colour, specially evolved for spatial colour studies. In focus was the difference between colours selected and colours perceived, and the differences between the two rooms. Colour shift was assessed with the aid of a *method for colour matching* and is displayed using direction arrows on a colour hue circle. The characteristics were described verbally, touching upon both colour and spatial perspectives. Perceived colour and colour character serve jointly to provide an experience of the entire situation. Phase 1 is described in paper 1, "Colour Appearance in Different Compass Orientations" and in paper 2, "A Method for Comparison of Colour Appearance in Differently Illuminated Rooms."

1.4.2 Phase 2, Red-Green Investigation

Would the same hue shift tendencies in the room with yellow and blue colours also occur with red and green colours? Red and green hues were included in the investigation so that all the elementary colours were present. A supplementary study was carried out where the most significant features were the same as in phase 1:

- Investigations were exploratory.
- Experiments were carried out in full-scale rooms with windows facing north and south.
- Daylight was transmitted through double-glazed fully transparent windows, and with the selected colour on all four walls.
- The same method for colour matching using a colour reference box was employed.
- Hues and nuances were selected on the same principles.
- Room colour shift was related to chosen inherent colours.
- A descriptive, reflective method was used for verbal descriptions.

The intention of describing colour as phenomenon and experience was the same as in phase 1, but greater emphasis was put in phase 2 investigations on what was experienced – both colour experience and spatial experience. I used more observers, partly in order to carry out a greater number of studies, and simultaneously to test methodology. Data were processed with statistical methods for rational treatment, and in order to relate the information to component factors. The red-green investigation was described in four part-studies oriented towards colour in north and south-facing rooms and focusing on:

- Perceived colour, hue shift and colour experience.
- Perception of colour and spatial character.
- Emotions brought about by room colour.
- Differences in emotional experience resulting from differences in size of colour surface.

These phase 2 studies are described in papers 3, 4, 5 and 6. The study relating to perceived colour and verbal colour description in full-scale rooms is presented in paper 3, "Study of Colour Shifts in Various Daylights." The identity colour of the rooms is compared and any colour shift assessed in terms of hue and nuance. Verbal colour description using own words is supplemented with colour impression. Paper 4, "Significance of Colour in Spatial Character," deals with spatial experiences relating to room colour and compass orientation. Differences in spatial character due to compass direction and colouring are assessed with the help of semantic differentials and verbal description. Paper 5: "Colour Emotion in Full- scale Rooms" accounts for a study of the emotional effect resulting from room colour and compass orientation. Emotional effect is investigated using a method for primary emotions. Where applicable, the results were compared with a study by Oberascher and Gallmetzer, 2003. Paper 6: "Colour Emotions in Larger and Smaller Scale," a study with semantic differentials relating to character of rooms in the various colours, is compared to the Swedish contribution to an international project carried out with small colour samples (Billger et al 2002).

2. THEORETICAL POINTS OF DEPARTURE

Both feelings and colours are psychological phenomena, experiences in the soul/mind. Thus it is hardly strange that connections exist between those parts of the brain "creating" colours and the locations for our emotions. One

> may even assume that feelings and affects may be triggered by colour stimuli prior to colours being identified as such. For in fact connections exist between retinal colour receptors and ancient locations in the brain for our emotions. This direct line of contact was of course useful in individuals being able to "act quicker than the passage of thought" in cases where colour entailed danger. (Sivik 1995 p. 36)

Hesselgren (1954, 1964, 1969, 1987) systematised existing research relating to sensory experience via sensory impression, something he entitled 'sense modalities'; and he constructed models for how these impressions or perceptions led to specific predetermined sensory experiences via human physical constitution. He wrote that colour gives rise to feelings and contains qualities enabling people to attach connotations between colour and internal and external things: *we attach significances to be understood as superior integrated wholes. The significances are mostly loaded with feelings to a greater or less extent, and the significance spreads throughout the thing concerned (Hesselgren* 1964 p. 233*).*

Hesselgren worked at charting structures between form and expression by giving visibility to patterns between form and perception. Through this he was able to show how form could be read as an expression of transferred significance. This ultimately concerns symbolism and associated meanings. In order to distinguish form (colour) and content, Hesselgren (1987 p. 41) used the terms *formal characteristics* and *formal aesthetic*. Formal characteristics were chromatic qualities of surfaces or visual fields such as yellowness and redness, while formal aesthetic denoted aesthetic evaluations of sensory perception *at the bottom of every complex sensory experience*, such as beautiful forms and colours. This included associations to colour or the additional term connotations. Thus form relates to sensory perception while content relates to everything else in a sensory experience in its entirety. Hesselgren's theory of perception, with its phenomenological method and application to colour and form, has influenced me.

Hesselgren conducted several investigations on relations between the built environment and sensual experiences, and in order to look into the experiences of humans he used a model for *primary emotions* by psychologist and researcher

Plutchik. This method was formulated back in 1962, and Plutchik then further developed the ideas himself along with other theoreticians (Ekman, Friesen 1978; Ekman, Davidson 1994; Plutchik, Kellerman 1980, 89). In short the method involves noting defined emotions on a differential scale of five. Plutchik defined eight emotions that he felt were universal and primary. Most adults are acquainted with these irrespective of culture and education. Plutchik originally listed what he considered to be primary emotions in an evolutionary perspective. In 1989 he listed the set of emotions I have used: joy, acceptance, surprise, expectation, anger, fear, sadness and disgust (Plutchik 1962, Plutchik and Kellerman 1980, 1989).

2.1 Colour Concepts and Definitions

My concern has been to try to pinpoint the colour as it appeared in the room as well as to capture the sensory experiences emerging from the situation. In my research I have used Hesselgren´s models for sensory experience and in *this context,* turned it to colour experience. Sensory is denoted as *involving or derived from the senses, to perceive, feel. Sensory channels relating to or concerned in sensation from the sensory organs in the sensory cortex.*

The term 'experience' was used throughout the project*: colour experience and spatial experience.* Colour experience relates to a reaction to or effect from the sensory characteristics of colour, what in day-to-day life is called emotion. This experience or feelings may consist of memories, associations and metaphors. I use 'experience' as an overall term covering sensory impressions relating to the entire situation, both space and colour. Experiences were investigated using several methods, including verbal description. To cover the relation between colour and observer's emotional response English interchanges the terms colour emotion, colour semantics, colour meaning and colour association. Ou (2004) recently suggested that these fields of research have become mixed, and suggests that *colour emotion* should be reserved for research treating human emotions arising in connection with colour impressions. *Colour semantics* should instead denote fields of research dealing with the significant of and association to colour. Thus in the method description, I use the terms 'colour semantics' and 'colour emotion' separately.

The term 'gestalt'[4] was used in paper 1 but it did not feel adequate enough in describing groupings arising from statistical analyses in paper 4. From there on I have chosen to use the more everyday term *character.* With character I refer to 'some' common category of perception in relation to *spatial character*. The term 'gestalt' did not feel adequate enough in describing groupings arising from statistical analyses.

2.1.1 Perceived and Inherent Colour

During the project the term *colour appearance* has been used in my papers. Colour appearance is a wide- spread concept used to signify the performance of a colour in an arbitrary situation. At this point though, I have determined to use the term *perceived colour* instead of *colour appearance*. The term 'perceived colour' was defined to further emphasise colour as perception (see Hård & Svedmyr 1995 p. 226). Green- Armytage has recently (2005) argued for clearer terminology, since the term 'colour' meant different things to different people in different fields, causing difficulties. He identified these areas of use and described seven different colour terms, calling them: Conventional Colour, Substance Colour, Formula Colour, Spectral Profile Colour, Psychophysical Colour, Inherent Colour and Perceived Colour. Colour appearance has also been used in highly controlled studies (Xiao et al. 2003, Chain et al 1999, 2001, Romero et al 2003) that have little in common with how individuals experience their environment. Billger and Fridell Anter (2006) continued the dialogue and established that Colour Appearance is used within research (CIE 2004)[5] in the development of colorimetric tri-stimulus values and chromaticity diagrams, which cannot be termed 'perceived colour' but are rather 'psychophysical colour'. At this point though, I determined to use the term *perceived colour* instead of *colour appearance*. The term 'perceived colour' was defined to further emphasise colour as perception (see Hård & Svedmyr 1995 p. 226).

Perceived colour: "the colour an observer perceives an object or a field to have in

4. Gestalt (from German: "guise", "form", "figure") is a limited, closed and structured entirety, the qualities of which cannot be reduced to the characteristics of its parts. Gestalt therapy and the term gestalt were described by Max Wertheimer in 1923 from a need to formulate human insights as wholes greater than their parts. Wertheimer formulated the terms fundamental to this field and six laws of gestalt: proximity, closure, similarity, good continuation, common fate, and symmetry.
5. CIE (Commission Internationale de L`Eclairage).

any given light and viewing situation".[6] A colour percept is not a constant characteristic, but rather a perception that varies according to the viewing conditions. This takes place via differences in light and shade and differences in sight organ physiology. I use the term 'perceived colour' in description and comparison of colours.

Identity colour is a colour term developed by Billger (1999 p. 23, 2006 p. 148), and is a variation of perceived colour. Identity colour is particularly useful in spatial colour studies and is defined as: *the main colour impression of colour units of a room that are perceived as uniformly coloured.* It is a term that corresponds to a holistic attitude: the colour we see in arbitrary visual relationships. Identity colour may be described through the *colour variations* arising in the sense of vision and in varying light conditions.

The term *inherent colour* was used as a base point for measuring differences that arose. Inherent colour refers to the colour a colour object would have if observed in standardised observation conditions as denoted for NCS colour samples in agreement with their specifications, i.e. with their colour code. This entails colour samples being placed at a 45° angle, observed in a light cabinet with simulated daylight consisting of six Luma Colorette fluorescent lights at 5,400 K (Hård 1995 bok 1, p. 74, Hård and Sivik 1981, Fridell Anter 2006 p. 140). Inherent colour is a constant characteristic independent of external circumstances, presuming requirements are adhered to. Inherent colour is compared to the *identity colour* that arises.

The difference between inherent colour and identity colour is a *colour shift*. This consists of a shift in both hue and nuance and is described according to its difference to inherent colour. In other cases the terms *hue shift* and *nuance shift* are used. (See papers 1, 3 and 4.)

Variations in weather or spectral distribution can cause rapid differences in hue and nuance within one and the same room. These variations in colour performance are entitled *colour elasticity* (Billger 2006 p. 147, Hårleman 2000 p. 79). (See paper 1.)

I use the term *breaking point* to denote a specified point in colour space where a general trend in shift stops and is replaced by a trend in another direction. Fridell Anter (2000 p. 106) has previously used it as a specified point in colour space where

6. Translation Fridell Anter, 2000 p 23.

the general shift tendency discontinues and the inherent colour and perceived colour coincide.

2.1.2 NCS Concepts in Short

I have used the NCS (Natural Colour System) colour notation system and colour terminology, and defined *colour* according to the NCS glossary. *Colour* is not measured wavelengths, but rather what we see as colour, and NCS is a method of describing colour perception.[7] The NCS system is based on the concept of common reference points for *elementary colours*, reference points with which every colour can be compared. In a three-dimensional model, a double cone, entitled the NCS Colour Space, all imaginable surface colours can be placed and thus given an exact NCS notation. In order to more easily understand the parts included in the NCS notation, the double cone is divided into two two-dimensional models, the NCS Colour Circle and the NCS Colour Triangle. The NCS- colour atlas is a collection of colour samples illustrating the underlying colour order system.

The hue of the colour you find in the *Colour Circle*, it describes whether the colour is a yellow or a yellowish red etc. The *Colour Triangle* is a vertical section through the colour space for the different hues. In the triangle you can find the nuance of the colour, which shows the visual amount of whiteness, blackness and chromaticness. (SCI 2004).[8] (Figure 4, The NCS Colour Circle and Colour Triangle.)

Colour: colour percept, colour perception, colour sensation; that which a human being in any given situation sees as colour and which makes it possible, primarily, to distinguish objects and fields using their colour differences (*colour discrimination*) and, secondly, to characterise objects and fields with the help of e.g. colour names (colour identification); the colour percepts can have different *modes of appearance* (*Färgordlistan*, Tonnquist 1995 p. 217).[9]

Elementary colours: colour percept that can be described only by reference to it-

7. NCS colour system, the relation between NCS notations and instrument-measured values and the colour atlas represent a Swedish standard since 1979. The colour atlas is used as an illustration of NCS colour notations.
8. SCI (Scandinavian Colour Institute) owns and administrates the NCS system. For further information relating to the NCS see SCI or NCS websites, own publications or other in-depth literature.
9. Translation Fridell Anter, 2000 p 23.

self. There are six elementary colours: white, black, yellow, red, blue and green. The first two are achromatic, the others chromatic. These six colours are also referred to as "psychological colour primaries" (SCI 2004).

Elementary attribute: the degree of resemblance of a colour to an elementary colour. The elementary attributes are: whiteness, blackness, yellowness, redness, blueness and greenness (SCI 2004). In the three-dimensional model named the NCS Colour Space, all imaginable surface colours can be placed and thus be given an exact NCS notation.

Hue: attribute of a chromatic colour percept expressing the degree to which it resembles one or two chromatic elementary colours. Colours with the same relation between the two chromatic elementary attributes are defined as having the same hue (constant hue). (SCI 2004)

Nuance: two-dimensional colour attribute that (irrespective of hue) expresses the relationship between whiteness, blackness and chromaticness in a colour percept.

In the Colour Atlas the colour samples are arranged and identified according to the colour order system. The Colour Circle illustrates the relationship between hues in the NCS colour glossary. The Colour Triangle illustrates the relationship between whiteness, blackness and chromaticness independently of hue. (SCI 2004)

Lightness: attribute of a colour element such that it appears lighter or darker than another colour element under the same illumination and viewing conditions. (SCI 2004)

2.2. Seeing Light, Colour and Light Colour

Colour may be dealt with from various angles, i.e. the physical (flow of electromagnetic radiation), the physiological (eye and sense of vision), the psychophysical, and the psychological (colour percepts) (Tonnquist 1995 pp. 23- 49). A number of models exist within psychophysics that describe colour in physical terms and which have little in common with colour as it is seen. As a visual phenomenon colour continuously works together with the physical, physiological and psychological aspects, which also may co-vary with one another. No simple connection exists between light emission and colour perception (Liljefors 1990, 1999, 2006 pp. 229-250). The colour of a surface is more closely related to e.g. composition of light emission across the emission's entire span. The spectrums of direct and diffuse solar radiation are continual (as fire and incandescent light) as opposed to other artificial lighting – entailing good opportunities for colour reproduction. An illuminated surface absorbs part of energy emission reaching it and reflects the remainder.

2.2.1. Signal Processing at the Retina

When this remaining energy meets the retina the physiological part of our colour vision commences. This vision is based on differences in the intensity and wavelength of physical light energy on the retina in a process of comparison. Light energy or photon flow is physically characterised by three qualities: *spectral distribution, intensity* and *direction of radiation.* There is great terminological confusion here, since *light* is used for both light energy and visual light, while many textbooks attempt to explain *visual light* as *visible light.* Liljefors suggests the terms $_{vis}$ and $_{phys}$ for possible use in differentiating between visual and physical aspects. All this is important to point out if we are to understand currently accepted ways of mixing up visual and physical perspectives. My thesis treats the visual aspect alone, thus no specific indication other than in this section is necessary.

The nature of *spectral distribution* in daylight$_{phys}$ is different in sunlight$_{phys}$ and sky light$_{phys}$. Although daylight$_{vis}$ is commonly considered as lacking colour$_{vis}$, it can often be described in terms of warmness or coolness; something that is felt rather than seen. These differences in the spectral distribution$_{phys}$ of light can result in surfaces showing different colours$_{vis}$ in differing situations. There is a natural variation in *intensity* of daylight$_{phys}$ during the day, and such differences have a considerable influence on how we perceive a colour$_{vis}$. Colour$_{vis}$ can change only through changes in the intensity of illumination$_{phys}$.[10] The chromaticness of object colours$_{vis}$ increases when there is an increase in illumination$_{phys}$, even when the spectral distribution of the light$_{phys}$ remains the same. This is particularly noticeable when we consider that colours$_{vis}$ are clearer and more chromatic on sunny days; "the world appears more colourful when the sun is shining". *Direction of radiation* is also of great import on how we

10. See Bezold-Brücke and Abney in section 2.3.2.

perceive colours$_{vis}$ in space. Our visual sense is highly sensitive to differences in lightness$_{vis,}$ and a varied light distribution$_{vis}$ helps us in our spatial interpretations. The direction of radiation and its distribution in space primarily describe the room and the light itself. *Visual connections* between different surfaces in a room have an influence on composition of light radiation, they contribute to room light colour$_{vis}$. In turn, room colour$_{phys}$ and composition of spectral distribution and light temperature interact with room colour$_{vis}$. Following processing in various ways by the layer of nerve cells on the retina, the information is conveyed to the optic nerve in the visual centre and the neurological process commences.

2.2.2 Interpretation Processes in the Brain

In order to see, physical visual information in itself is not enough – the information has to be interpreted. "The brain attempts to understand what has been seen, and here adds experiences, memories and feelings" (Liljefors [11]). The interpretation process contributes to what we see being highly composite and requires learning in early years. By studies of blind people who via operation have gained fully functional visual organs, it is known that interpretation processes have to include components that are learnt and without these physical visual information cannot result in what we mean by seeing.

For example, the brain conducts comparisons between juxtaposed surfaces, or between part and whole of field of vision (Liljefors 2006 p. 231). Thus the nerve impulses that commence along the optic nerve provide information on both spectral distribution and intensity simultaneously. The sense of vision works at comparing contrasts. This process is based on enhancing or reducing differences in relation to one another and thereby leading to colour phenomena$_{vis}$ such as contrast and assimilation. Enhancement of contrast signals takes place in specific situations. This enhancement effect is particularly strong where two different surfaces meet one another with sharp borderlines (Liljefors 2006 p. 236). If on the other hand the borders are diffuse and blurred then this effect of enhancement is reduced but still present.

11. In conversation in a pedagogic session, my translation.

Such enhancement effects are important to colour vision and comprise a decisive difference between human colour vision$_{vis}$ and colorimetry (psychophysical). Contrast enhancement (also termed 'induction') involves two colours$_{vis}$ influencing one another by enhancing the difference between them. Here we have simultaneous contrast and successive contrast with coloured afterimages. Assimilation is the opposite of enhanced contrast, as for example when neighbouring colours$_{vis}$ in a pattern, affect one another so that differences are reduced and they together form a new colour$_{vis}$.

The sense of vision does not passively register, but is highly active and selective. Only a portion of what we see is registered, the rest is filled in by two parallel systems – the boundary contour and feature contour systems (Davidoff 1991 p. 71). Terminologically there is a clear difference between perceived colour$_{vis}$ and experience of colour$_{vis}$ also at a purely physiological level. Through a visual categorisation of visual information the brain is activated via two separate pathways. Contact with the entry level makes available three distinct types of knowledge. One of them relates to the *sensory characteristics* of a surface and is termed *hasa* knowledge. This information may be expressed as red, light-red etc. The other pathway has *isa* knowledge and relates to *stored knowledge regarding function* and *associative comprehension*. (Davidoff 1991 p. 97, 145, 171). When this information is interpreted in the brain, the visual experience is enriched with feelings and memories. This is where the psychological aspect of colour vision begins. By providing what we see with interpretations we can see our surroundings differently and have recollections from different perspectives.

2.2.3 Colour of Light$_{vis}$

Uniform light$_{vis}$ distribution in a room can quite easily give it a monotone and cheerless quality. Liljefors and Sällström developed terminology concerning visual light to enable us to differentiate between physical and experiential dimensions of light colour (1979 p. 19). They write that we cannot see what spectral distribution light$_{phys}$ contains, but we still make a judgement as to the quality of the light$_{vis}$. The phrase 'light colour' is also the subject of terminological confusion and a mixing of entities of importance to the experience of colour in e.g. north and south-facing rooms. Liljefors and Sällström define the following terms[12] contributing to a development of vocabulary:

Light colour (Ljusfärg): observed colour$_{vis}$ of illumination; not only depends on type of light$_{phys}$, but also on the degree of other circumstances such as room colouring$_{phys}$ and lighting arrangement$_{phys}$. It also depends on the adaptation situation of the eye. Light colour$_{vis}$ is not normally experienced as chromatic, but rather greyish or more or less white. On the other hand it may be experienced as being able to give colour$_{vis}$ to objects in a room. Thus light colour experience can be described as giving the impression that colours look dulled or intensive. This is the visual dimension.

Light character (Ljuskaraktär): this relates not only to visual observation. When we talk about the "warmth" or "coolness" of light we express a broader observation, as might be made for a room in its totality. This assessment of light character is based on e.g. feelings and notions brought to life when an individual is confronted with (or exposed to, enclosed in) the light.

2.3 Current Field of Research

2.3.1 Semantic Differentials in Spatial Studies

A lot of colour research has been conducted using a method with semantic differentials. With the help of such graded differential scales it is possible to measure experiences and compare them to one another. Investigations have shown this method to be surprisingly reliable (Hogg et al. 1979, Küller 1995, Sivik 1995). By using statistical analysis methods, the meaning variables of the scales can be grouped and condensed in greater entities or factors. In 1957 Osgood et al. showed that three factors independent of one another form the root for the majority of descriptive words: value, activity and potency. The meaning variables of differential scales have been put to the test by many researchers down the years. They revealed that these belong to different factors depending on field of investigation. However, one value factor and one factor for activity or potency recurred in most compilations. Hogg et al. (1979) found five factors relevant to colour in spatial models: *dynamism, spatial*

12. Two terms are presented. The third term, Type of light (Ljusart): can involve a basic classification of different light sources, such as warm white and daylight-like strip lights. Type of light represents the physical dimension, and is not relevant here.

quality, emotional tone, complexity and *temperature*. In my investigation I used all these factors excepting *complexity* in the study relating to room character. (Paper IV). In 1975 Küller produced the SMB method[13] to describe built environment with the aid of semantic differential scales. SMB is an established method used in many spatial studies, but as an architect I chose to draw up other variables for spatial experience since I felt the need for better-adapted variables (See paper 4).

Kobayashi (1981) investigated how people experienced individual colours or colour combinations and developed the Colour Image Scale method. He constructed semantic spaces for colour significance with the aid of semantic differentials and statistical methods. Kobayashi found that the warm – cool meaning variable was related to hue, soft – hard was related to value,[14] while clear – greyish was related to chroma.

Sivik (1970) conducted numerous studies on the meaning conveyed by colour in relation to associative meaning variables and with the help of semantic differentials.

Sivik and Taft (1989, 1992) continued research into the associative meanings of colour combinations. They organised semantic spaces where relations between significances and colours could be established. Among other things, their work resulted in structured analyses of semantic aspects of colour experience. By this they identified the characters of colour combinations. Such characters vary since object of investigation and individual variables affect the factors. The warm-cool meaning variable is an example of a sensorial emotion. Sivik investigated the charge of this feeling held by individual colours and ascertained that not only colour hue was significant, but also nuance (Sivik 1995 p. 48). Many studies have been conducted without a monitored interplay between comparable colours. According to Sivik's comparative investigation in Greece and Sweden, both Greeks and Swedes describe the relationship between colour and this meaning variable in similar ways. As expected, the warm maximum was in the yellow-red and red areas, and the cool maximum in blue and blue-green. Greater whiteness correlated with coolness and greater chromaticness with warmth.

13. *Semantisk Metod för Bostadsforskning* (Semantic method for building research).
14. *Value* helps us to discriminate a light colour from a dark colour (Tonnquist 1995 pp. 99-100).

2.3.2 Colour Phenomena in Various Illumination

The French chemist Chevreul was a forerunner who was early in his studies of visual colour differences in yarns and woven fabrics. As head of a Jaguard textile mill he received complaints from customers that they had ordered yarns and these had been interchanged since colours of the woven fabrics did not correspond to their expectations. Following thorough studies he found how the colours affected one another and wrote down principles for various contrast phenomena such as simultaneous contrast. He also studied other colour phenomena in different illumination. Chevreul illuminated his colour samples with daylight, sunlight and diffused sunlight, but not skylight. The colours showed themselves differently depending on distribution of direct and diffused illumination. He found that chromatic surfaces illuminated with sunlight had more clear colours, while corresponding surfaces with diffused daylight tended towards blue-grey (Chevreul 1839).

The Bezold-Brücke effect is known since 1931. This involves differences in illumination intensity causing hue shift. The study related to spectral colours, i.e. confined to energy from a narrow band of the radiation spectrum. In other words, the same spectral distribution with increased illumination intensity causes a hue shift from red and yellow-green towards yellow, while violet and blue-green shift towards blue. Lower illumination intensity causes a shift from yellow towards red or green and from blue towards green. This means that yellow and blue prevail in strong lighting and red and green in reduced lighting (Derefeldt & Berggrund 1994 p. 22). The Abney effect, known since 1910, means that greater illumination intensity also has an effect on colour samples through an increase in sample chromaticness. Yellow, the least colour intense hue, at the same time reaches its maximum in greater intensity of illumination compared to the other hues. If, however, illumination intensity is increased when the point of maximum chromaticness has already been reached, then the result will be a whitish perceived colour. In this way both low and high luminance cause chromatic stimuli to appear achromatic[15] (Davidoff 1991 p. 79). (Figure 7.)

15. Black, white or grey.

Hård et al (1983) have made a series of tests comparing colour samples in various types of conventional illumination. The tests were conducted indoors with colour samples arranged at 45° angles in a light cabinet. The investigation showed that within separate parts of the colour world various types of illumination caused different degrees of shift in both chromaticness and hue. When illumination was changed from simulated daylight 5400 K to incandescent lighting, the perceived colours of yellow-green, green, blue-green and part of blue samples shifted towards blueness. In the case of red-blue, red-yellow and yellow colour samples, the perceived colour shifted instead towards red. This small colour shift signified two areas for breaking points: green-yellow and yellow-red. The nuance changes were small for weakly chromatic colours, but the tendency towards greater chromaticness was clear among more chromatic colours. When instead illumination was changed from incandescent light to 3000 K warm-white standard strip lighting, hue shift for specific groupings of colour was significant. Indications now existed of four areas where direction of colour shift was replaced by a different direction: between green and yellow, between green and bluish green, between reddish blue and violet, and between violet and red (Svedmyr 1995 pp. 90-92). (Figure 8.)

Billger conducted a similar experiment with her colour reference box. The intention was to investigate the function of the colour reference box in relation to the observer being adapted to two light situations, firstly the lighting in the box and secondly the lighting in the room in which the box is positioned. The question was: could the adaptation be assessed and controlled. In one study simulated daylight 5400 K was used in the room, and 40 W incandescent light was used in the box, resulting in a two-directional shift in hue: one direction from bluish red to red and one from reddish blue through an uncertain passage near to elementary blue, over green, yellow, and towards orange. This shift involved two areas of breaking point: violet and orange (1999 Paper 4, p. 18). (Figure 9)

Using natural daylight, Fridell Anter has compared inherent colour and perceived colour on facades. The investigation compared perceived colour in for example three different types of daylight: sunlight, light from clouded sky and light from a clear sky. In general, perceived colour was found to be more chromatic and more whitish than inherent colour. There were also great differences in tendencies between different areas of colour, two directions for hue shift were reported, corresponding well with Billger's with areas of breaking point at violet and orange. It was obvious that diffuse light gave greater blackness than direct sunlight. Fridell Anter also found signs indicating that the diffuse light could cause a hue shift from yellow towards blue and an increased chromaticness for bluish colours (2000 p. 152). (Figure 10.)

Despite colour and light being so interwoven, perceptual differences exist between colour and light experiences. Billger (1999, paper II p. 38) found that it is possible for individuals to compensate for colour differences resulting from varied luminance, but not colour differences caused by reflection. That is to say, a colour sensation is normally recognised despite a different illumination, but on the other hand this recognition is not present to the same extent for reflected colour sensations. Fridell Anter (2000, p. 167) claimed that in certain circumstances it would be better to talk of experiencing light difference rather than colour difference. Such a delimiting of the term 'colour' is to be found in interpretation itself of the situation: whether or not the subject experiences the sensation as colour or light.

The relation between illumination and colour has been studied by a great many researchers. A lot of studies have been done using colorimetric tri- stimulus values and chromaticity diagrams that describe visual impressions. Other studies have been carried out in laboratories in highly specialised conditions such as light consisting of a single wavelength. Some researchers have used daylight and different models of calculation to describe the colour of objects (Romero et al 2002) or the characteristics of daylight in differing circumstances (Chain et al 1998, 2001). In one study simulated daylight and CWF lighting was used in combination with colour patches of different sizes to accomplish a rooms study (Xiao et al 2003). The limited number of spatial colour studies in daylight relevant to my work, are presented below.

2.3.3 Spatial Colour

Chevreul (1839) also studied colour and some of its spatial relations, such as coloured surfaces placed at angles, or three-dimensional objects such as vases, coats or skeins with formations of light and shadow. Due to the lack of a standard perceptual system of colour description and methods of describing perceived colour, his studies could only result in proximate tendencies. Minah (1996, 1997, 2002) studied the function of colour in cityscapes, its influence on the entirety and how the colour of individual facades appears depending on weather and viewing distance. Minah claimed that colour is of great significance to architecture by colour contrasts and spatial effects creating figures and backgrounds in the cityscape experience. The job of colour in the design process is to clarify, supplement and emphasise, rather than be an independent commentary, he wrote. For Minah, chromaticness was seen to be more important than hue and abiding nuance with regard to visibility in the cityscape, both in clear and overcast weather. Strongly chromatic features appear closer, the light-dark contrast in bright weather is important to the visibility of specific buildings since black dominates up towards the sky and white in the cityscape.

Billger's research has been of particular importance to me since she has worked with perceived colour and colour shift in full-scale rooms. Billger (1999) developed methods and terminology for the study of colour in rooms, and she also developed the colour reference box in order to allow comparison of perceived colour in different rooms using a colour matching method (Billger 1999, Billger and Hårleman 1999). Billger also initiated the term *identity colour* especially for spatial colour studies. Indeed, in detailed viewing, a room displays numerous colour variations. I used the colour reference box, the colour matching methods and the term *identity colour* and colour variations in my studies. See paper 2, "A Method for Comparison of Colour Appearance in Differently Illuminated Rooms".

A further endeavour is seen in the work of Smith in relation to colour and design processes. Smith's (2003) starting point was the term 'place', which designers see in four contexts as object, product, communicator or social domain. Designers who look upon *place* as an experience or social domain formulate their task differently to those who treat it as an object merely to be coloured. Smith ascertained that architects and designers worked with colour intuitively, not making use of existing knowledge, with colouring often being left to the youngest employees. The conclusion is that the ability of colour to give expression could be used far more effectively in our environmental colouring.

2.3.4 Colour Emotion and Colour Design

Despite numerous pertinent studies in colour appearance and colour emotion having been conducted in recent years, only a few of these are relevant to research in architecture (Billger & Fridell Anter 2006). Three of these accounted for concern colour emotion, and were conducted with similar methods and achieved similar results. Oberascher & Gallmetzer[16] (2003) and da Pos & Valentini (2005) used Ekman's seven basic emotions: *happiness, surprise, anger, fear, sadness, disgust*, and *contempt*. Basic emotions are derived from mimic emotional expressions, and defined as not reducible to others (Ekman & Friesen 1978). Basic emotions differ from Plutchik's primary emotions in that they form two positive[17] and five negative categories (primary emotions: four positive and four negative).

Da Pos & Valentini (2005) found *happiness* and *surprise* to be positively bright emotions, relating to lighter – and in the case of *happiness* to more yellow – colours than the other emotions. They write nothing on the chromaticness of selected colours, keeping to hue and achromatic shade. They also found that *fear and the other dark emotions* related to colours inclined to blue and red and in general more purplish colours than the other emotions, corresponding well with the results of Oberasher & Gallmetzer where *contempt* relates to grey, blue and purple, with sadness relating less to yellow than disgust.

Da Pos & Green- Armytage (2006) excluded contempt and used only six basic emotions in their study. Three clearly marked groups were found with regard to lightness of colour samples: *happiness, surprise* and *fear* related to very light colours, *sadness* and *disgust* related to an intermediate group and *anger* to relatively dark colours (usually black and red).

As far as chromaticness is concerned, *sadness* and *fear* related to very slightly chromatic colours (close to 0.0). While *happiness, surprise* and *anger* associated to strongly chromatic colours. According to them, this suggested that the latter three emotions were *active* and the former *passive*. The most recurring colours in their studies were

16. Oberasher & Gallmetzer used *pleasure* instead of *happiness*, from Ekman & Davidson, 1994.
17. Neither Ekman nor Plutchik distinguish between positive and negative emotions. I make the distinction here to ease comparison of models. In basic emotions *joy* and *acceptance* are combined into one. Happiness and *expectations* are not included, but *contempt* is.

within the yellow-red quadrant, indicating that active emotions show a warm appearance. Surprise, sorrow and fear were relatively whitish, while anger was strongly blackish. Level of blackness for surprise and happiness was low, while orange was strong.

Oberascher & Gallmetzer (2003) suggested a colour - emotion classification: black = sadness; yellow = pleasure; red = anger; brown = disgust. They summarise their conclusions: *A room decorated in tones of yellow and orange, for instance, will tend rather to evoke pleasure for the majority of people in our culture than a black and grey room. Black and grey generally have an oppressive effect. The combination of black and red tends to have a menacing effect. Pink tends to evoke aversion and rejection, but in its ambivalence – not only in the USA – it also appears as a favourite colour, especially for women, according to Heller, even taking a fourth place, with 8 %, after blue, red and green.*

Sivik (1995 p. 50) has pointed out the difference between studies involving the direct effect of colour and those relating to colour associations and opinions on their psychological effect. The four studies mentioned above relate specifically to colour associations, thus one cannot be sure that these results can be used to reach conclusions on effects in spatial situations. This can be seen in comparison between one of my studies and two other studies (Oberascher & Gallmetzer 2003, Ou et al 2005). See paper 5 and 6.

3 METHODS OF INVESTIGATION AND ANALYSIS

3.1 Common to Phases 1 and 2

Qualitative methods were used with own-word description, also with use made of associations that turned up in the situation. I was inspired by a phenomenological outlook and found support there for use of an exploratory method with colour as experience and a phenomenon conveying significance. Presence in the daylight-illuminated rooms with their colours triggered an event belonging to the phenomenon colour that could not be omitted.

Two main methods were used for assessment and comprehension in both model and full-scale studies: one method for describing perceived colour, and one method for describing the experience of spatial character with a descriptive and reflective technique. In total 191 full-scale studies were carried out in the project with 79 observers in realistic spatial situations. Rooms facing north and south were recurrently painted and compared to each other and to colour samples. The terms inherent colour and identity colour were used in analysis of room colours. The perceived colours were assessed using NCS terminology using the terms hue, chromaticness, blackness and whiteness. The method for colour matching aided by the colour reference box was used in all comparative observations.

Table C. The studies in figures.

	Phase 1	Phase 2
	Yellow-blue	Red-green
No. of colours	12	13
No. of observers	7	72
No. of studies	73	118

Colour matching is an established method for comparison of colour samples against a standard[18] (Hård, Sivik, Svedmyr 1995, Billger 1999). This method has been developed in order to manage comparative studies between inherent and perceived colour. Such a method, using a colour reference box, was used throughout the project. The colour reference box was developed to allow colour studies to be conducted in a simple manner, without trained observers, so as to compare colour impressions between rooms in various illuminations. The colour reference box has its own illumination, thus colour samples displayed had the same illumination in both rooms. The procedure was that observers compared the colour they saw on one or several walls in each room with colour samples placed in the colour reference box by the project leader. The colour samples were changed according to observer directions until colour matching was achieved. Sample colour code was then recorded. An interpolated colour code was recorded in cases where no specific colour sample matched the wall colour but where the observer otherwise felt it to be found in the colour space

18. *Colour matching* is a term used in quite a different way in other research fields such as: (1) mixing wavelengths in cones and rods, or tri-stimulus values in colorimetry, (2) mixing stimuli colour to achieve a similar percept (a standard).

between two or three selected colour samples. On completion of one room study, the box with its illumination was removed to the next room. This is a relative method, i.e. the colour data cannot be taken as absolute facts, but the method maps out the relation between the situations. There are indeed no perfect methods and that is why I have used many different methods and use a comparative analysis.

Observers had the task of considering each room and colour in an aware and attentive manner. Observer instructions were found in questionnaires that also contained room for recording assessments. A construction cabin was used as experiment room with gables in a north-south direction. The cabin had windows in each gable and daylight was transmitted through uncoated double-glazed windows.

3.2 Phase 1, Yellow-Blue Investigation

A dividing wall did not bisect the construction cabin that was used in phase 1, instead one of the windows was covered alternatively. In that way, the internal space was illuminated as either a north-facing or south-facing room. Three yellow and three blue hues in two nuances were used totalling 12 inherent colours. The hues were: greenish yellow (G80Y), yellow (Y) and reddish yellow (Y20R) greenish blue (B30G), blue (B) and reddish blue (R80B). The nuances were: one whitish (1010) and one more chromatic nuance (1030). (Figures 11 and 12.)

The studies in phase 1 were observed for a lengthier period than those in phase 2. A fuller description is to be found in paper I. Practised observers were used, architects with training in NCS terminology and interest in colour research. The reason for that was that methods and questionnaire were under development and I wanted observers with interest in colour, space, and training in NCS terminology. (See appendix A, Questionnaire in phase 1). The methods for assessment and understanding were:

Methods for judging the perceived colour

(1) Colour matching using a colour reference box.

(2) Visual Evaluation of the light situation.

Methods for assessing the experience with a descriptive, reflective technique

(3) Verbal description of colour impression.

(4) Verbal description of colour character

(5) Semantic scales relating to room atmosphere.

Other methods of analysis

(6) Watercolour painting

(7) Memory colour

(8) Colour scheme

(1) Method for *colour matching using a colour reference box* (Billger 1999, Hårleman 2000). Colour samples were placed in the colour reference box, one at a time, and wall identity colour was described by comparison to selected inherent colour. The box had the same illumination in both rooms – D65 lighting – and thus functioned as a standard situation. In visual comparison the colour sample was then chosen that was most like the wall colour. This method is presented in greater depth in paper 2.

(2) *Visual evaluation* in order to observe the distribution of the types of light and colour in the rooms.[19] This method can be used to study the effect of physical factors on what we see. The method uses seven factors: *light level, light distribution, shadow, reflexes, glare, light- colour and colour* (Liljefors 2006, Billger 1999, Hårleman 2000).

The section for assessment of the experience began with a method for (3) *Verbal description of colour impression* using own words. As stated earlier, I also used the terms 'identity colour' and 'colour variation' to describe colour perception in spatial situations. A method for (4) *Verbal description of colour character* was used for describing rooms and colours with observers own words. The words were enumerated and categorised before being compared with assessments of other rooms and colours. (5) *Semantic scales* in three steps were constructed for evaluation of atmosphere in each room.

Analysis was based on alternate comparison with the different methods. One (6) watercolour painting was made by myself. Completing the second study (7) the identity colour in the current room was compared with the one from the former. A (8) colour scheme was made, a simple outline investigating the effects seen in *Visual evaluation*. This method showed to be of great importance in analysis. (Figures 5 and 6).

19. Method for *Visual Evaluation* developed by A. Liljefors and J. Ejhed 1990, also described in Liljefors 1996.

3.3 Phase 2, Red-Green Investigation

The investigation with red and green inherent colours was broadened to describe both colour and spatial experience. A greater number of studies were carried out with a greater number of observers. Methods were further developed and semantic differentials introduced. Data on character of rooms was processed using SPSS statistical methods [20] and then used in analyses of relations between spatial character, hue, nuance and compass orientation.

A new experiment cabin was divided into two rooms, each with a window, one with window facing north, and one with window facing south. As previously, daylight was transmitted through clear, double-glazed windows. The inner walls of the rooms had a glass-fibre textile; window framing was painted white, while floors had a beige plastics floor covering. Compared to the positioning of the cabin in the yellow-blue investigation, the cabin was positioned with more grass and bush in the south and more tarmac surface in the north. Several of the observers remarked on a light reflection from surrounding yellow facades towards the afternoon in the north-facing room. (Figure 3.)

Three red and three green hues in two nuances were selected, with one later omitted. Thus six red and five green colours were used in total, along with a previously used yellow and blue. The hues were yellowish pink (Y80R), pink (R) and bluish pink (R20B), and bluish green (B70G), green (G) was in two nuances, whitish 1010 and more chromatic 1030. Yellowish green (G20Y), reddish yellow (Y20R) and reddish blue (R80B) were in the 1030 nuance only, a total of 13 inherent colours. (Fig 4. Colours selected for phase 2)

Seventy-two observers were used: 52 students of architecture and interior design, and 20 professional architects and interior designers. In all 118 studies were carried out. The observers performed each room study individually, with each one taking approximately 30 minutes. Observers were told to take their time, to make an acquaintance with the colours, to dwell in their experience and then formulate it. A questionnaire was used. (Appendix B, Questionnaire in phase 2).

20. Software, acronym for Statistical Package for the Social Sciences.

Methods for judging the perceived colour

(1) Colour matching using the colour reference box as in phase 1.

(2) Verbal description of hue and nuance.

(3) Memory matching with pre-selected colour samples.

Methods for assessing the experience using a descriptive, reflective technique

(4) Method for visual evaluation.

(5) Verbal description using own words of experience of colour and room.

(6) Semantic differentials [21] with regard to room character.

(7) Semantic differentials with regard to colour emotions.

Methods for analysis

(8) Tabulated data from colour matching

(9) Statistical methods as factor analyse, t-tests and two-way analysis of variance.

(10) Verbal descriptions

(11) Comparison with other studies.

The chief method of judging the perceived colour was (1) colour matching using the colour reference box. Chief method for assessing the experience of the room was the (4) visual evaluation. In order to describe (5) general initial impressions of colour and room, own words and associations were used and this was followed by use of semantic differentials. The following experiential factors were used in scales on (6) room character: *spatial quality, emotional tone, dynamism and temperature.* [22] Two new ones were tested: *embracing* and *uplifting*. I used eight primary emotions to describe (7) colour emotion: *anger, joy, acceptance, surprise, fear, sadness, disgust and expectation*.

Inherent colour notations were related to room orientation and results were analysed with (8) tabulated colour data. Data concerning the room character were analysed with (9) statistical analyses and comparing (10) verbal descriptions. The results concerning primary emotion were (11) compared with two studies in colour emotion: Oberasher and Gallmetzer (2003) and colour emotion made with small colour samples Ou et al (2005). Similar inherent colours and emotional variables were compared.

21. A differential scale has zero in the centre and two bipolar words. The scale used here is of the Likert type.
22. These are Hogg's original factors, and the fifth is complexity.

4 DISCUSSION ON RESULTS

This is made up of discussions relating to various observations in the project as well as some of the methods used.

4.1 Observations

I observed in phase 1 that changes in perceived colour in daylight, frequently had a cyclic progression, i.e. *colour elasticity was often cyclic*. Variations in light were not seen other than as differences in perceived colour. This was visible in the rooms as transient variations or as more persisting somewhat longer periods. This meant that room identity colour varied in cycles around inherent colour, as lighter or darker, more or less chromatic and with greater or lesser hue shift. Normal oscillation was 10-30 steps in whiteness, blackness and chromaticness with inherent colour as base. For example it could be darker and more reddish or brighter and less chromatic. (See papers 1 and 3)

Besides the cyclic variations in the rooms, clear patterns for colour shift between rooms depending on quality of daylight could be established. Light quality differences due to compass orientation caused clear and well-documented shifts in hue and nuance from inherent colour to identity colour. These shifts were regular and not difficult to anticipate. The embracing form of the rooms also resulted in a different nuance that was also easy to anticipate. In general, identity colour was less whitish and more chromatic than inherent colour. Also, both nuances, the whitish and the more chromatic, had separate patterns for colour shift. The more chromatic 1030 nuance became still more coloured, increasing in chromaticness up to 20-40 steps.[23] The whitish 1010 nuance increased in chromaticness by only 10 steps, but instead had the greatest hue shift, from inherent colour to identity colour. Direct sunlight in the south enhanced the chromaticness and also shifted yellowish hues towards elementary yellow. The diffuse sky light in the north enhanced the chromaticness of green, blue and red hues. In this light all these shifted towards elementary blue. On the other hand, yellowish colours were reduced in yellowishness, becoming less coloured with a trace

23. Mean value 5-20 steps.

of greyishness and a tendency towards green or pink, depending on colour attribute of inherent colour. Inherent colours with an elementary yellow hue became greenish yellow and the reddish yellow became orange or pink (Papers 1 and 3).

4.1.1 Significance of Colour on Spatial Character

Different colours leave different impressions; they spark off different associations and are described with words covering personal domains. When using the method for *describing colour impressions with own words* it was found that colours with the same elementary characteristics brought about impressions common to the majority of observers. These colour impressions were described consistently with a small number of words used regularly within a specific area of colour. Each elementary attribute appeared to be reserved for a special domain described with words mutual to one another. The elementary qualities were described with individual sets of words. *Soft* was clearly reserved for yellowish and bright identity colours, whereas bluish and blackish identity colours were described as *strong* or *potent*. Pink (1030-R) was frequently described as *loud*, especially if bluish (1030-R20B). Yellowish pink (1030-Y80R) on the other hand could be described as *charming* or *irritating*, but never as loud (See paper 3).

The clear expressions for colour connotations that arose in descriptions with own words followed the same pattern with semantic scale. Green was associated with nature and failed to spark off anything like the powerful reactions seen with pink. One observer recalled with a sighing voice a tedious childhood stay in a hospital; otherwise the reactions were of quiet, calm and natural life. Pink was almost always commented on exterior to questionnaire. Pink aroused clear feminine associations and observers established themselves as for or against the colour quality pink. At the same time as the more chromatic pink (1030-R) could be described as *warm*, *youthful* and *relaxing* in the south-facing room and *alive* and *mature* in the north, it could be a provocative room colour. No other room colour was described with anything like the same charged intensity. These rooms could be described as *unrelenting* and *irritating* and the north-facing ones as *loud* and *even more irritating*. Common negative words for pink rooms were *loud*, *glaring* and *harsh*. Why do all pinkish colours spark off such powerful feelings? The fact that they do is the primary argument for the different hues having different connotations. Pink is a colour that at least in our part of the world is associated with *skin, face, body* and *femininity*. Certain nuances of pink (yellowish pink) resulted in a feminine impression that could be associated with and described in terms of *girlish*, while pink without yellowishness could gain the descriptive word '*brothel*'. Pink was frequently described with words relating to closeness: bodily, spatial and emotional. The bodily association could be both secure closeness (pink and whitish pink) and to a varying degree an unrelenting closeness. Since pink rooms related to skin and face, certain rooms (yellowish pink) were associated with love, while others (bluish pink) instead could be associated with *affect* depending on face colour. The blackish pink identity colour could furthermore be associated with *absence* and *neglect*. The yellowish rooms were most frequently experienced as soft, but the room with the brownish yellow identity colour was consistently described as *heavy*. The south-facing rooms in reddish yellow became so strongly chromatic that they could be experienced as a *bodily mass*, a *closeness that was exacting*. My conclusion is that *negative judgements could be due to them not looking soft enough* (See paper 4).

How the observers experienced the rooms varied entirely in relation to the identity colours. It was striking how closely reactions followed differences in hue and nuance. The perception of warmth increased considerably with yellowish hues and pure pink. The colours of bluish pink and bluish green were seen as emanating the most coolness. It was clear that pink and green were experienced as opposites to one another. While pink was perceived as lively, cheerful, embracing and the least formal, green was perceived as tranquil, open, formal and hard. Just as Liljefors and Sällström (1979) talked about light character, one can also talk about colour character. *Colour character relates to an experiential dimension; a colour character that pays regard to space as an entirety, with feelings and notions brought to life when one is exposed to or enwrapped in a prevailing* colour. (Liljefors, Sällström p. 20)

The terms warm and cool colours are well established and well-known. In full accordance with this concept, somewhat yellowish colours were found to be warm, and bluish colours were perceived as cool. Despite this, the extremes – warmest warm and coolest cool – were not the same for all the observers. The warmest and coolest hues and nuances varied while the actual colour field was the same. Most observers saw yellowish red in a colourful nuance as the warmest colour. More difficult was appointing the coolest colour, between reddish blue, elementary blue or greenish blue. Pale greenish blue was found to be the coolest. The sensation that certain colours were approaching or receding, were also confirmed. The south-facing rooms with warm colours gave a powerful impression of approaching close to observers, just as the cool colours in north-facing rooms clearly receded in the way that they made the walls appear further from observers (See papers 1 and 4).

4.1.2 Colour Emotion

Rooms in warm, yellow and pink colours were more liked than rooms in cool, green and blue colours. This was somewhat surprising, since architects are considered to appreciate cool colours to a greater degree than other professional groups (Janssens 1984). Also, the warm colours caused stronger emotional effects such as happiness and approval than the cool colours, as well as considerable anger and sadness. The negative emotional effects were strongest with cool colours, these causing fewer positive emotions and higher scores for the negative, topped by disgust and contempt. The whitish nuance made a slight impression, with the stronger 1030 nuance giving a stronger impression, including with emotions other than those for the 1010 nuance (See paper 5).

4.1.3 Comparison of Two Colouring Methods

I have compared the results from the two opposing methods for colouring in order to see if one of them is perceived as more positive than the other. The principle in one case is to enhance the light situation by room colours, the other means counteracting or neutralising.

- The enhancement method – bolstering light situation – was most popular for warm colours in the south. This combination resulted in most happiness. The least popular combination was cool colours in the north rooms.

- The neutralising method – counterbalancing light situation – was more popular with warm colours in the north rooms than cool colours in the south rooms.

One single warm colour (reddish yellow) was highly popular in the north rooms. In general, cool colours in the south rooms were popular – with acceptance greater being than happiness (See paper 5).

4.2 Methods of Investigation

The exploratory character of the project, with numerous different methods, was important. The objective after all was to record the experiences and associations observers had with colour and rooms that were not entirely easy to put into words. Nor does the opportunity normally present itself to take a pause and do this. The basic method for colour description using the colour reference box gives precise NCS notations for expressing identity colour and colour shift. Perhaps these are too precise – such exact notations, that despite all must be adapted to each given situation, can be alluring. The qualitative methods presented sensitive descriptions and variables for describing and comparing both rooms and colours. Finally, the collaboration between all the methods used showed how well perceived colour was in accord with recorded NCS notations.

A further vital quality of the project was its being conducted in full-scale rooms. Model studies can be used for tracing tendencies in hue and nuance shifts, but full-scale rooms brought about clearly more intensive colour experiences. It is less than certain however that a comparable study would achieve the same results in model and full-scale. As far as colour semantics are concerned, the embracing form of rooms is probably of still greater import. Using the statistical methods, new meaning variables could be tried out and developed. The variables *uplifting*, *hard/coarse* and *embracing* were shown to be relevant and important for description of room experience.

4.2.1 Colour Reference Box and Adaptation Effect

The colour reference box generated concordant data showing trends in agreement with results from other methods in the project. The box is still being developed, and it was important to test it in a 'standard situation'. The issue was whether light prevailing in the room where both box and observer were present could influence the appearance of a colour sample in the box. After all, observers were adapted to room light situation and not to colour reference box light, something that could have presented itself as a serious problem. Adaptation to actual light situation is important, and here there were two light situations. It was necessary to look into the adaptation effect to see if this could constitute a systematic error. Billger developed a method to test the degree of accuracy a practised observer could identify colour sample NCS codes. This test was carried out in both the north and south-facing rooms using the NCS method.[24] The observers cited two inverse situations that were selected for investigation. One involved a room painted in a warm colour (reddish yellow) in direct sunlight, making the box light look cool. In the other situation the room was painted in a cool colour (reddish blue) and illuminated with a cool north light, giving box light a warm appearance. Possible adaptation effects in use of the colour reference box are discussed in paper 2: *A Method for Comparison of Colour Appearance in Differently Illuminated Rooms*. We used data from the research of Billger and myself and made comparative studies of inherent colour in various situations and with differing methods. A preliminary model is presented for use in small adjustments of colour data.

Paper 2 contains details of how colour matching with the colour reference box entailed minor adaptation effects in certain situations. Such situations – with major differences between light in box and light in room – an adaptation effect was detected. Since a reddish yellow room (1030-Y20R) in sunlight has a strong increase in chromaticness and yellowness, box colour sample will instead appear less yellow. Through this observers might compensate their visual impression by selecting a colour sample that despite all matches the colour of the wall. In such cases the colour reference box fails to function as a standard situation identical to both rooms and which the colour sample refers to, measuring instead the light differential between room and box. This adaptation effect can be calculated and adjusted, and was furthermore negligible in the majority of daylight studies. The situations where it arose were not ignored indeed observers reacted to the difficulty in colour matching in such differing illumination (See paper II). Though the occurrence of adaptation effects still

24. The NCS method constitutes a description of hue, chromaticness and blackness in NCS terms using own assessment. The method is based on the assumption that our elementary colour reference is identical to all. See 2.1.

cannot be excluded. Therefore, dominant methodology has been to use several methods for description and comparison. Observer's descriptions of colour experience serve as illustrations of support or rejection of colour data. Those, and further on as a source for descriptive words can also be very useful in further research.

4.2.2 Comparison Between Phases of the Project

Since light radiation into buildings is highly sensitive to a series of meteorological factors, besides room location, each experiment is strictly speaking circumstantial. Hence specific rooms cannot be expected to be purely identical despite same compass position of windows. In this way, data from phases 1 and 2 from the investigation could not be brought together as though the experiment rooms were identical. *Despite this it is clear that the main tendency between the compass points remains.* After all, the greatest perceptual difference in the project was between room inherent colours and not between rooms with the same inherent colours. The differences between a red and a green room in the same compass orientation compared to two rooms in the same red inherent colour are of course greater. On the other hand small tendency differences were found between both phases. Tendencies in the north-facing room were the same: from yellowish inherent colours in two directions from an area between yellow and reddish yellow. One of the directions was towards yellow, from yellow to green and from green to reddish blue. The other direction was from reddish yellow towards red and from red on towards reddish blue. The difference between the two phases of the investigation was displayed as several possible breaking points in the south-facing room. Two examples:

- In phase 1 *greenish yellow* tended towards yellow. *Greenish yellow* was stable in phase 2, i.e. inherent colour and identity colour were the same. On the other hand, green tended towards bluishness, mildly indicating a breaking point between yellow and yellowish green in the south room.
- In phase 1 blue and *greenish blue* tended towards greater greenishness. In phase 2 the tendency of *bluish green* was towards greater greenishness while *green* tended towards blue, indicating a possible breaking point between greenish blue and bluish green.

This result was unexpected. It could not have been due to weaknesses in either method or observer groups since the descriptions were unanimous. One possible reason could have been differences in experiment room localisation in relation to surroundings. A further possibility is that colour shifts towards greater yellowishness in south-facing rooms express themselves in this way, like tidal waters pulling yellowish hues with them. The hue shift towards greater yellowishness in the room with windows facing south went in two directions from the area with pale yellowish inherent colours, yellowish pink and yellowish green. The yellowish pink colour area coincided with other research on artificial light (Billger 1999) [25] and natural daylight (Fridell Anter 2000).[26] Inherent colour and identity colour were one and the same in the yellowish green colour area. A possible explanation here is the observation by Romero et al (2003) that colour variations in red-green direction depend on the yellowish or bluish proportion of the coloured object. As stated earlier, the tendency between north and south compass points remains. On the other hand, localisation of the south-facing room may have been decisive in determining exact breaking point of tendency, when between yellow and green and between green and blue. *Thus tendencies between room compass orientations can represent a more important clue when predicting a perceived colour than when attempting to denote exact breaking points* (See papers 1 and 3). Additional studies are required here for south-facing rooms. Reddish blue in north and south-facing rooms in phase 1 revealed no stable tendency for colour shift. Inherent colour in both rooms was alternately perceived as more reddish or more bluish. On the other hand, in phase 2 a tendency towards greater reddishness in the north and reduced reddishness in the south was noted. It is likely in this case that the hue of the inherent colour coincided with the wave range of the light radiation. Since reddish blue is found at reciprocal ends of the wavelength, with violet at the shortwave side and red at the long-wave side, small variations in incident light will be expressed with greater clarity with this inherent colour. Perhaps room lightness is the hue determinant – the brighter the room the more red, the darker the room the more blue (See papers 1 and 3).

25. Billger 1999a, page 18, and 1999b.
26. Fridell Anter 2000, page 107.

5 CLOSING COMMENTARIES

A Regular Colour Shift

A regular pattern for colour shift between compass points can be ascertained. The different light qualities in the rooms resulted in differences in identity colours and breaking points. The yellowish colours in south-facing rooms appeared deeper in colour. In the north-facing rooms yellowish colours appeared less yellow: they became less deeper in colour and instead more greenish, brownish or pink. The nuances used had their own, clear patterns of colour shift. The rooms with the whitish nuance 1010 changed most in hue, while the more chromatic nuance 1030 became still more intense.

Colour Connotations

Hue and nuance include powerful colour connotations. Spatial perception was firmly linked to identity colour, and distinct colour connotations were attached to the colours. The various colour areas had their own domains from which associations arose. Pink and green practically resulted in opposing spatial characters where light colour contributed to spatial experience as an adjustment of the associations. Pink is associated with facial colour, physicality, human closeness and femininity, while green associates to nature, openness and relaxation. In cases where the light situation opposed such associations, opposites within the same domain appeared instead. *Warm* and *cool* were the most distinct variables.

Differences in Spatial Character

Light quality in rooms resulted in differences in spatial character. North and south-facing rooms had, to a limited degree, differences in spatial character; the north- facing room had a less elevating character. Effects from the different colours override difference in location. As the colour in each room is evaluated it can be expressed as enhancing or reducing the colour attributes, and the connotations attached to the colours.

Full-Scale Studies

Full-scale studies are a better means in investigating experience of interiors than are room models. This relates not only to size of colour samples used, but also the embracing quality of rooms and the opportunities for observers to gain access to associations and impressions that arise through their presence in built rooms. The colour reference box revealed itself to be a highly useful aid in room studies since it generated reliable data even with a small group of observers. Three new variables were developed for experience of spatial character. The methods used made it possible to develop new variables for a more finely tuned description of how rooms and colours are experienced. These new variables are: uplifting, hard/coarse and embracing. The investigation has paved the way for a fresh perspective on spatial colour experience. Large quantities of data were assembled together to produce a larger composite outline, making it easier to understand the links between recorded perceptions on a scale and visual colour.

5.1 NEW ISSUES

Several interesting questions for future research have taken shape during this project:

1. Comparison between colour reproduction in natural daylight and the most recent generation of artificial daylight.
2. Continued investigation into verbal descriptions and colour domains.
3. Testing of other hues and nuances. I used a limited number of hues, but further colours need to be tested if we are to find out more about location of breaking points. Where exactly are the breaking points in different nuances?
4. The hue shift that was discernable in the south-facing room was surprising and hence worth a further study. Could the case be that more than two breaking points in the hue circle exist within one and the same nuance?

6 REFERENCES

Billger, M. 1999. *Colour in Enclosed Space*. Gothenburg, Chalmers University of Technology, Form och Teknik. ISBN 91-7197-820-8.

Billger, M. 2000. Evaluation of a Colour Reference Box as an Aid for Identification of Colour Appearance in Rooms. *COLOR Research & Application.* Vol. 25 (3) June, 214-225.

Billger, M. and Fridell Anter, K. 2006. An architectural understanding of colour research. *AIC proceedings, South Africa.*

Billger, M. and Hårleman, M. 1999. A method for comparison of colour appearance of differently illuminated rooms. *CIE Proceedings, Warsaw CIE publication* 133, Vol. 1, Part 1, 67-71.

Billger, M., Stahre, B. and Konradsson, Y. 2002. Colour emotions in Sweden, in Sato and Hansuebsai, *Proceedings for the International Conference on Colour Emotion Research and Application*, July 5-7, Chulalongkorn Univ. Thailand; 1-3.

Burns, S. A., Elsner, A., E. Pokorny, J. and Smith, V. C. 1984. *The Abney effect: Chromaticity coordinates of unique and other constant hues*. Vision Research 24, Issue 5, 479-489.

Chain, C., Dumortier, D., and Fontoynont, M. 2001. Consideration of daylight's colour. *Energy and Buildings*, 33, 193–198.

Chain, C., Dumortier, D., and Fontoynont, M. 1999. A comprehensive model of luminance, correlated colour temperature and spectral distribution of skylight: comparison with experimental data. *Solar Energy, Elsevier Science Ltd*, Vol. 65, No. 5, 285-295.

Chevreul, M. E. 1967. *The principles of harmony and contrast of colors and their applications to the arts.* (1839). Introduction and explanatory notes by Birren, Reinhold Publishing Corporation, New York.

Davidoff, J. 1991. *Cognition through Color.* The MIT Press, A Bradford Book, Cambridge, Massachusetts.

Derefeldt, G, and Berggrund, U. 1994. *Färg som informationsbärare (Color as a conveyor of information).* (Stockholm, Sweden: Defense Research Establishment, FOA).

Ekman, P. 1992. An argument for basic emotions. Cognition and Emotion. 6, 129-

200.

Ekman, P. and Davidson, R.-J. 1994. (Ed.) *The nature of emotion.* Oxford University Press: New York.

Ekman, P. and Friesen, W.V. 1978. Manual for Facial Action Coding System. *Consulting Psychologists Press: Palo Alto.*

Fridell Anter, K. 2000. *What colour is the red house? Perceived colour of painted facades.* Doct. Thesis. Royal Institute of Technology, KTH, Stockholm. Trita Ark-2000:4, ISBN 91-7170-595-3.

Frizell, B and Löfberg, H.A. 1970. Dagsljus inomhus. Swedish. Statens institut för byggnadsforskning. T 11.

Green- Armytage, P. 2006. The value of knowledge for colour design. *Color Research and Application* 4, pp. 253-269.

Hesselgren S. 1987. *On architecture : an architectural theory based on psychological research.* Lund: Studentlitteratur, ISBN: 91-44-24021-X; Bromley: Chartwell- Bratt ISBN: 0-86238-094-4.

Hesselgren S. 1969. *The Language of Architecture.* Studentlitteratur, Lund.

Hesselgren S. 1954. *Arkitekturens uttrycksmedel : en arkitekturteoretisk studie med tillämpning av experimentalpsykologi och semantik.* Doct. Thesis. Swedish. Almqvist & Wiksell, Stockholm.

Hogg, J., Goodman, S., Porter, T., Mikkelides, B. and Preddy, D.E. 1979. Dimensions and determinants of judgements of colour samples and a simulated interior space by architects and non- architects. *British Journal of Psychology,* 70, 231-242.

Honkonen, V., 2003. In VV2, Visuella världar, Vessel, G. http://www.visuellavarldar2.se. Swedish.

Hopkinson, R.G., Petherbridge, P., Longmore, J. 1966. *Daylighting.* University College, London and Building Research Station, England.

Hård, A., Sivik, L. and Svedmyr, Å. 1983. *Belysning och färgseende II. Undersökning av färgade föremåls olika färg under tre vanligen förekommande ljuskällor*. Swedish. Färginstitutet. Färgrapport *F23*, ISSN 0280-2198 11-17.

Hård, A., Sivik, L. 1981. NCS - Natural Colour System: A Swedish standard for colour notation. *COLOR Research and Application,* 6 (3) 129-138.

Hård, A. 1995. Det naturliga färgsystemet, in *Färgsystemet NCS: tanke, tillkomst, tillämpning. Färgantologi bok 1*. Swedish. Byggforskningsrådet, Stockholm. ISBN 91-540-5694-2.

Hård, A., Svedmyr, Å. 1995. *Färgsystemet NCS: tanke, tillkomst, tillämpning. Färgantologi bok 1*. Swedish. Byggforskningsrådet, Stockholm. ISBN 91-540-5694-2.

Hårleman, M. 2000. *Färg i norr och södervettande rum. Kulörtonförskjutning genom varierande ljusförhållanden*. Swedish. KTH, Stockholm. ISBN 91-7170-590-2.

Janssens, J. 1984. *Looking at buildings – individual variations in the perception of building exteriors.* School of Architecture, Lund Institute of Technology, Lund.

Kobayashi, S. 1981. The Aim and Method of the Color Image Scale. *COLOR Research and Application, John Wiley & Sons, Inc*. Vol 6, No 2. Summer, 93-107.

Kunishima, M. and Yanase, T. 1985. Visual effects of wall colours in living *rooms. Ergonomics, vol.* 28, No 6, 869-882.

Küller, R. 1995. Färgens inverkan på människan, *in Färgantologi bok 2, Upplevelse av färg och färgsatt miljö.* Swedish. Byggforskningsrådet. ISBN 91-540-5696-9.

Kuller, R. 1991. Environmental Assessment from a Neuropsychological Perspective, in Gärling, & Evans (eds), *Environment, Cognition and Action. Oxford University Press*, Inc. New York. 111- 146. ISBN 0-19-506220-5.

Kuller, R. 1980. Architecture and emotions . In Mikkelides, B. (ed), *Architecture for People. Holt, Rinehart and Winston,* New York. ISBN 0-03-057491-9.

Küller, R. 1975. *Semantisk miljöbeskrivning.* Swedish. Psykologiförlaget, Stockholm.

Liljefors, A. 2006. Ljus och färg i seendets rum, in *Forskare och praktiker om Färg Ljus Rum.* Swedish. Fridell Anter (ed.), Forskningsrådet Formas, Stockholm, Sweden. ISBN 91-540-5966-6.

Liljefors, A. 1999. *Seende och ljusstrålning : baskompendium.* Swedish. ALV Belysningslära, KTH. Stockholm.

Liljefors, A. and Ejhed, J. 1990. *Bättre belysning: om metoder för belysningsplanering*. Swedish. Statens råd för byggnadsforskning. T17. ISBN 91-540-5207.

Liljefors, A. and Sällström, P. 1979. *Ljusfärg som belysningskvalitet.* Swedish. Statens råd för byggnadsforskning, Stockholm. Rapport R 146. ISBN 91-540-3143-5.

Löfberg, H. A. 1976. *Dagsljus utomhus, grundläggande samband och tillämpning-*

sexempel. Swedish. Byggforskningens informationsblad B 9. ISBN 91-540-2635-0.

Minah, G. 2002. Color constellations in the Seattle cityscape. *Proceedings SPIE 4421*, 146 http://spiedl.aip.org/scitation

Minah, G. 1997. Figural Color in the Seattle Cityscape. *Proceedings, AIC Color 97*, Kyoto: Color Science Association of Japan.

Minah, G. 1996. Reading Form and Space. *Architectural Design*, Academy Group Ltd. Vol. 66, no 3/4.

NCS colour terminology http://www.ncs.se

NE, Nationalencyklopedin, 1994. Swedish.

Oberasher, L. and Gallmetzer, M. 2003. Colour and Emotion. Psychology of Architecture and Design. *Proceedings, AIC 2003.* Bangkok.

Ou, L.C. ,Luo, M. R.,Woodcock, A., Billger. M., Stahre. B., Huertas. A., Dinet. E., Richter. K. and Guan. S. 2005. The Effect of Culture on Colour Emotion and Preference. *Proceedings AIC Colour 05-10th Congress*, Granada.

Ou, L. C.: *Definition of Colour Emotion*, 2004, online http://colour-emotion.co.uk/whats.html

Ou, L.C., Luo, M. R., Woodcock, A. and Wright, A. 2003. A Study of Colour Emotion and Colour Preference. Part I: Colour Emotions for Single Colours. *COLOR Research and Application,* Vol 29, Issue 3, 232-240.

Osgood, C. E., Tannenbaum, P.H., Suci, G. J. 1957. *The Measurement of Meaning*. Urbana, University of Ill. Press.

Plutchik, R. 1962. *The Emotions: Facts, Theories, and a New Model*. New York.

Plutchik, R. and Kellerman, H. 1980. *Emotion : theory, research, and experience*. New York: Academic Press.

Plutchik, R. and Kellerman, H. (Eds.)1989. *The Measurement of Emotions.* New York: Academic Press.

Da Pos, O. and Green- Armytage, P. 2006. Colours and basic emotions. *AIC proceedings, South Africa*. 89-92.

Da Pos, O. and Valentini, S. 2005. Colouring the emotions. *AIC proceedings, Granada, Spain.* 263-266.

Publication CIE (International Commission on Illumination) 2004. *A Colour Appear-*

ance Model for Colour Management Systems: CIECAM02. 159.

Rasmussen, S. E. 1957. *Om att opleve arkitektur.* Gards, Köpenhavn. In Danish.

Rasmussen, S. E. 1959. *Experiencing architecture*. London: Chapman and Hall.

Romero, J., Hernandez-Andrés, J., Nieves J. L. and Garcia, J. A. 2003. *Col. Res. Appl.*, 28 (1) 25-35. Online.

Rudberg, B. 1993. *Statistik*. Swedish. Studentlitteratur, Lund. ISBN 91-44-37701-0.

Sato, T. Kajiwara, K. Hoshino, H. Nakamura, T. (2000) Quantitative evaluation and categorising of human emotion induced by colour. Adv Colour Sci Technol; 3:53-59.

SCI 2004 NCS Atlas SS 19102:2004. Stockholm .

Sisefsky, J. 1995. *Om färg, uppfatta, förstå och använda färg*. Swedish. Skandinaviska Färginstitutet, ICA Förlaget AB, Västerås ISBN: 91-534-1557-4.

Sivik, L. 1995. Om färgers betydelse, in *Färgantologi bok 2, Upplevelse av färg och färgsatt miljö.* Swedish. Byggforskningsrådet. ISBN 91-540-5696-9.

Sivik, L. 1970. *Om färgers betydelser*. Swedish.Färgrapport F09, Skandinaviska Färginstitutet, Stockholm.

Sivik, L. och Taft, C. 1992: *Colour combinations and associated meanings – semantic dimensions and colour chords.* University of Gothenburg. Gothenburg's Psychological Reports. Volume 22 No 1.

Sivik, L. och Taft, C. 1991. *Semantic variables for the evaluation of color combinations – An analysis of Semantic Dimensions.* Göteborg Psychological Reports, Volume 19 No. 5.

Sivik, L. och Taft, C. 1991. *Dimensions of color combination meaning in relation to characteristic color chords.*

Sivik, L. och Taft, C. 1989. *Semantic Variables for Judging Color Combinations – An analysis of semantic dimensions*. Göteborg Psychological Reports, Volume 19 No 5.

Smith, D. 2003. *Environmental Colouration and/or the Design Process.* COLOR Research & Application, Wiley Periodicals, Inc. Volume 28 No. 5, October.

Tonnquist, G. 1995. *Färgsystemanalys. Färgantologi bok 3.* Swedish. Byggforskningsrådet, Stockholm. ISBN 91-540-5696-9.

Xiao, K., Luo, M. R., Li, C. J., Rhodes, P. A. and Taylor, C. 2003. Specifying the

Colour Appearance of a Real Room. *The 11th Color Imaging Conference, IS & T and SID,* Scottsdale, Arizona. November, pp. 308-312.

7. OTHER LITERATURE

Bennet, T. J. A. 1988. *Aspects of English Colour Collocations and Idioms*. Carl Winter Universitätsverlag, Heidelberg. ISBN 3-533-03947-1.

Berlin, B., and Kay, P. 1999. *Basic Colour terms. Their Universality and Evolution*. CSLI Publications. Leland Stanford Junior University, USA. ISBN 1-57586-162-3.

Borg, A, (ed.) 1999. *The language of color in the Mediterranean: an anthology on linguistic and ethnographic aspects of color terms.* English and French. Almqvist & Wiksell, (Stockholm, Sweden. Stockholm Oriental Studies 16.

Byrne, A. and Hilbert, D. 1997. *Readings on Color, Volume 2: The Science of Color.* MIT Press. ISBN 0-262-02424-1.

Caivano, J. L. 1998. Color and Semiotics: A Two-way Street. *Color research and application* Vol. 23, nr. 6 Dec.

Derefeldt, G., Swartling, T., Berggrund, U., and Bodrogi, P. 2004. Cognitive Color. *COLOR Research and Application. Wiley Periodicals,* Vol. 29, No. 1, February.

Gage, J. 1998. *Colour and meaning. Art, science and symbolism.* Thames and Hudson. London, England. New ed. (California: University of California, 1999).

Gavel, J. 1997. *Colour. A study of its Position in the Art Theory of the Quattro- & Cinquecentro*. Almquist & Wiksell International, Stockholm, Sweden. ISBN 91-22-00296-0

Gilchrist, A. L., (ed.) 1994. *Lightness, brightness, and transparency.* Lawrence Erlbaum Associates. Hillsdale, New Jersey, USA.

Hardin, C. L. 1988. *Unweaving the Rainbow.* Hackett Publishing Company, Cambridge. ISBN 0-87220-039-6.

Hardin, C. L. and Maffi, L., eds 1997. *Color categories in thought and language.* Cambridge University Press. ISBN 0-521-49693-4.

Hutchings, J. B. 2003. *Expectations and the food industry. The impact of color and appearance.* Kluwer Academic Publishers. New York, USA.

Kay, P., and Maffi. L. 2000. Color Appearance and the Emergence and Evolution of

Basic Color Lexicons. *American Anthropologist* 101 (4) pp. 743-760.

Janssens *J. 2001. Facade Colours not just a Matter of Personal Taste- a psychological account of preferences for exterior building colours, in* Nordic Journal of Architectural Research *2, 2001.*

Nassau, K, ed. 1998. *Color for science, art and technology.* Elsevier. Amsterdam, The Netherlands.

Steinvall, A. 2002. *English Colour Terms in Context.* Doct. Thesis. Umeå universitet, Sweden. ISBN 91-7305-226-4.

Porter, T., and Mikkelides, B. (eds.) 1976. *Colour for Architecture*. Van Nostrand Reinhold, New York.

Taft, C. 1997. *Generality aspects of color naming and color meaning.* University of Göteborg, Department of Psychology. Gothenburg, Sweden

Tillberg, M. 2003. *Coloured Universe and the Russian Avant- Garde. Metiushin on Colour Vision in Stalin's Russia 1932.* Doct. Thesis. EIDOS No.10, Konstvetenskapliga institutionen, Stockholms universitet, Sweden. ISSN 1650-5298. ISBN 91-7265-683-2.

Zanjonc, A. 1993. *Catching the Light*. The Entwined History of Light and Mind. Oxford University Press, USA. ISBN 0-553-08985-4.

Valdez, P. and Mehrabian, A. 1994. Effects of Color on Emotions. *Journal of Experimental Psychology: General*. American Psychological Association, Inc. Vol. 123, No. 4, 394–409.

Wierzbicka, A. 1990 The meaning of color terms: semantics, culture and cognition. *Cognitive Linguistics* 1–1, Walter de Gruyter. Pp. 99-143.

8. LIST OF FIGURES

**The colour floats in the air
hit by sunbeams.
the colour closes.
and its surface creases.
displays dents
of the cloud**

Light, greenish yellow (S 1010-G80Y) before thunder

as a fully inflated balloon
A cloud drifts by and
Suddenly the balloon shrinks
Now the soft surface
where the heaviness
is reflected.

PAPERS 1 – 6

Colour Appearance in Different Compass Orientations

Hårleman, M.

Published in Nordic Journal of Architectural Research, 2, 2001.

1. INTRODUCTION

Imagine that we are walking along a corridor, glancing into the rooms on each side. Instantly we can see that the colours of the walls are not the same, even though we assume that they were similarly painted. At first, we might think that this is a mistake, or even a failure. Again we assume that the architect intended the same hue and shade on both sides of the corridor. Or we might think that it is agreeable with a natural variation in colour, a variation that in fact tells us about time and compass orientation. Alternatively, we might suggest that the architect should avoid such colour design, by giving the rooms on each side of the corridor colours of different hues.

Colour appearance differs in rooms facing different compass orientations. Divergences in light and situation make a distinction between rooms facing north and rooms facing south depending on sunlight and diffuse daylight. This is a well-known phenomenon, causing problems in making colour design. The problem is that we lack the knowledge to predict how different compass orientations influence colour appearances in different rooms. It is a design problem that makes it difficult to achieve a planned result. The problem is to foresee how the colour of light can affect colour appearance. How do we work with design in relation to rooms facing north or south? Is it possible to make a room with a " cool atmosphere" look warm and, vice versa: to make a warm, sunny room look cool?

Working as an architect, one still has to gain knowledge of colour appearance by trial and error. Some intentions of colour design fail during the learning period, and result in disappointing and poor colour designs. To rectify failures in large building projects costs a lot of money, of course, and is seldom done. On account of this,

I wanted to learn about colour appearance in daylight in general, and in north- and south- facing rooms in particular. The driving force was to carry out systematic studies in favour of design knowledge. I found that Billger had developed concepts and methods for colour research in enclosures.[1] She has broadened the field of colour research from colour samples into concerning colour appearance in rooms. Now it is obvious that this can result in knowledge otherwise not obtainable without the specific study of rooms. Billger made studies in artificial light and I made this investigation around daylight conditions. We have had a close collaboration and also used each other, and other colleagues, as observers. Beside shifts in hue and nuance I wanted to discover how people responded to the colours involved and to the character of the room. As common strategies in colour design are either to enforce or counteract the light, the strategy is in itself interesting to evaluate as well.

In this article I first sketch out some divergences between north and south, warmth and coolness. Thereafter follows a presentation of my empirical research, briefly on methods used and finally some research conclusions.

2. AN EVALUATION OF NORTH- AND SOUTH- FACING ROOMS

A room's compass orientation establishes conditions for experience. At first there is of course the matter of sunlight and diffuse daylight. In my research I use the word sky- light as a term for diffuse daylight. The motive is a need to separate between two kinds of daylight with differences in light distribution, light level, and spectral distribution. These contrasting conditions are differently processed, not proportionally, in the visual system. [2] The visual process affects contrasts as to either diminish or enhance them, like in assimilation and contrasting effects. The contrasting conditions also form impressions with other qualities, different experiences of room and colour.

Sky- light illuminates the north facing room together with reflections of both sunlight and sky- light. North-facing rooms have a relatively steady light level, with diffuse light and a good colour rendering. Therefore, sky- light is used as a standard model

1. Billger, M.: 1999. Amongst her methods and concepts I have adopted the Colour Matching Method with the Colour Reference Box as well as the Identity Colour.
2. Liljefors, p. 151. 99.

in specifications for artificial light. Rooms to the north are often thought of as being pleasant, with a greyish, dim light and a steady light level. However, while some people see sky- light as a neutral light, others see only cool light and a cool room character. Facing north, sunlight is seen mostly in the landscape outside, while the interiors rest in quiescent shade. Facing south, sunlight illuminates the whole interior and that result in a different expression. Sunlight, sky- light, and reflections from outside illuminate the south facing room. As clouds pass by, sunlight flickers and changes. It points out conditions of living life, such as time and weather. Clouds and atmospheric variations change, and this shows in colour appearance. In these rooms we can feel time fly, together with changes in mood. As if it was at random, we are given sudden moments of joy, but also sequences of long lasting monotony. Some of us experience discomfort in viewing conditions and burning heat in sunlit rooms, some only comfort. Hue and nuance undergo changes. Without knowledge about colour appearance in natural daylight we cannot control colour design. How do these differences affect colour appearance?(See figure 1.)

I have chosen to experiment with rooms facing north versus rooms facing south because they can be experienced as almost opposite to each other, both in how colours are perceived and how we experience the whole situation – the character of the room. This investigation is made in Stockholm, Sweden, and it concerns mainly observations on clear days, since fully overcast weather makes colours appear the same in all directions. Yet studies from all sorts of weather were made.

3. A STUDY ON COLOUR APPEARANCE: AIMS IN THE INVESTIGATION

The aim was to investigate how colour appearance differs between north- and south facing rooms. The investigation had three aims:

- The first aim was to describe shifts in hue and nuance with regard to the compass orientation of interiors. By this it would be easier to accomplish a desired colour design in a planned room. Facts and figures of predicted shifts in hue and nuance could help in colour design in general.
- The second aim was to examine and discuss different ways to work with colour design in various lighting conditions. Architects and designers often use two contradictory methods, either to counteract or to strengthen the light situation.

Because of this it is essential to know if it is possible to counteract the colour of light. Is it possible to make a room with a "cool light character" to be experienced as "warm", and vice versa? In order to evaluate this matter, it is important not only to ask, "what colour is it?" but also "what does it look like"?

Answering the first question one might say "blue", and the second "cool", "vibrant" or " receding." More knowledge in valuations like these can help to bridge the gap between a planned design and the result. From the view of an architect and designer, it is no use studying a colour without connection to a thing and/or a situation. This brings us to the third aim of this study.

- The third aim was to describe the room and its character in terms of colour and light. In a room, colour has a close relationship to its location. Therefore it is important to look at the situation as a whole, including both colours and room. This third aim was less studied than the other two, but still deserves to be mentioned. In this article, room character is defined as the subject's experience of the appearance of room, colour, and light in combination. Beyond an experimental situation, colour instead is merely a background in the room as a whole. A room consists of both physical elements, light and colours, by which it gains its character. As humans we react to the situation as a whole and relate colour, climate, light, and appearance to an experience of reciprocal actions. Here questions of a total appearance belong. Again, it is important to treat the question of what the colour looks like, apart from hue and nuance: the experience of a character as an added consideration.

4. TERMINOLOGY

- *Colour variations*: are defined as the local colour appearances of the identity colour. These differences might depend on light distribution, reflections from other surfaces and contrast effects.[3]

3. Billger, 1999, p. 11.

- *Identity colour*: is defined as the main colour impression of surfaces or parts of the room that are perceived to be uniformly coloured.[4]
- *Inherent colour:* the colour that the colour object would have, if it was observed under the standardised viewing conditions that are a prerequisite for the NCS colour samples to coincide with their specifications.[5] I quote Fridell Anter: This means that the inherent colour is a constant quality of the object and does not depend on external conditions (apart from bleaching, pollution, and other physical changes of the object itself).
- *Visual Evaluation*: is a method for visual evaluation of light and room to specify both physical and visual aspects of the light situation. The method is designed to establish and evaluate those connections.[6]

5. METHODS IN THE EMPIRICAL RESEARCH

My research is based on an empirical investigation of experimental character made with comparative methods in north- and south facing rooms. The overall research objective is to describe what happens with colours in various lights, not really why it happens. Observations are made using *room models* and *full-scale interiors*. The investigation is qualitative, with a perspective based on perception and phenomenology. The designer's perspective is taken as a starting point. Shifts in hue and nuance differing from the *inherent colours* are in focus, together with the colour gestalt and room character. The questions involved have two perspectives; what does the colour look like in the room and what does the room look like in the colour? A total of 126 studies were made: 43 studies of room models and 83 full-scale studies. Six methods for assessment and description have been used. In the investigation we have been working with two perspectives of attention, *the colour perspective* and

4. Ibid. The concept of identity colour did not work out properly in this study, probably because the identity colour does not cover the range of colour variations that are significant for these spaces.
5. Fridell Anter, 2000, p. 24., The standardised viewing conditions are defined as: • light booth with simulated daylight, 6x20 watt Luma Colorette flourescent tubes, colour temperature approximately 5400K, diffused through a opaline plastic sheet which gives approximately 1000 lux. • measurements of the light booth specified, its walls light grey with specified luminous refectance. • the colour sample to be observed measures 6x9 cm and is placed on a white panel with specified luminous reflectance, tilted about 45°. • the sample is viewed at approximately 90°, from a distance of about 40 cm.
6. The method is developed by Liljefors, A. and Ejhed, J, 1990, and in Liljefors 1996.

the room perspective. The colour perspective aimed at describing, in our own words, the experience of a colour in the specific room situation. This perspective demands a certain amount of time, as in experiencing a work of art. Through the colour perspective the colours were looked upon as a colour gestalt. In addition to this, the observers used a verbal description, exemplified with expressions as brilliant, dull, beautiful, glaring, full or pushy. The room perspective belongs to the total experience of room, colour, and light. In this lies the difference between a colour sample and the same inherent colour in a room where enclosure, shadows, distances, light and different light reflections together form a compound experience.

In the introductory room studies of model rooms, I used 3 yellowish and 3 bluish colours in two nuances of chromaticness; one was a pale nuance, the other was and a more chromatic one. These studies were fruitful and I decided to go on with the same inherent colours in the full-scale studies. (See figure 2)

The observers made several observations each, out of 12 inherent colours. Room models were used mainly to test concepts and methods. The room model was made of white cardboard with a "window" facing north respectively south, with a carefully arranged window at the side for observations. All four walls were painted in the same inherent colours, one at the time. The model had a grey painted floor in NCS 3000-N and white cardboard ceiling. It was made in a scale of 1:5, measuring 700 x 980 x 480 mm, the window for observations measuring 23 x 28 mm. For full-scale studies a building site shed, with one window in each short side, facing north and south was used. The shed measured 8, 40 x 2, 90 meters. The floor covering had a beige plastic surface and the ceiling was painted white. The walls had a coating in glass fibre textile and a latex paint, glare 7, was applied with a roller. Inside the shed, all four walls were painted in the same inherent colour. In experiments, one side was shut so that there was either sunlight or sky- light, alternatively.

For careful and conscious evaluation of colour and room, competent observers were used. All six observers were architects and four of them were colour researchers, used to assessing colour appearance, room evaluations and the NCS colour system. Observations were based mainly on two of those as permanent observers and for comparison; the other four observers were used on certain occasional studies. Notations were made on a form; descriptions in verbal while colour variations were marked on a sketch with an NCS colour notation. In an hour-long session of visual assessments, the observers commented on various aspects of the colour appearances, including impressions of change caused by atmospheric conditions. Six methods of observation were used. The observers evaluated the light situation by means of the *Method of Visual Evaluation.* A *Colour Reference Box Method* was used to gather data with a *Colour Reference Box*. *Psychometric scales* were used to describe the room character. An *Associative, reflective method* was used to describe colour response with verbal descriptions in the observer's own words. Between each change of inherent colour, a *watercolour painting* was made of both the north- and south facing room. In some cases, data from the studies seemed contradictory. To make an analysis, *memory colour* and *a colour scheme* were used together with these water- colour paintings. Put together, the colour scheme provided the missing link. In most cases this link proved that there where different sizes in area of distribution between some of the colour variations.

In assessing the light and colours in the room, the observers were guided by the questions in the form. They started with a holistic view of the situation as a whole, then shifted focus between colour variations, identity colour and room character. It was not required to use the different methods in a strict order, but I considered it of importance to commute between approaches to keep the vision vital. Secondly, they should evaluate the light situation with the Method of Visual Evaluation by Liljefors and Ejhed. This is made according to seven factors: lightness level, light distribution, shadows, glare, reflexes, colour of light, and colour appearance. The method in observing how room, colour and light interacted was essential. As this method was slow, it slowed down the overall pace and thus made it possible for careful observations.

In assessing colour appearance the Colour Reference Box Method by Billger was used. This method consists of a colour matching method using a Colour Reference Box.[7] The Colour Reference Box was set up with a standard source of illumination to provide

7. Billger and Häggström developed the colour reference box at Chalmers University of Technology. For detailed description and discussion about adaptatation effects, see Billger, 1999, paper 4. For further clarification " Assessing Colour Appearance in a Real Room Using Magnitude Estimation and Colour Matching Techniques" Billger in MPL Proceedings, London April 2000. Hårleman 2000, p. 29 and p. 87.

a reference situation, were NCS colour samples were illuminated and compared to certain areas on the walls. In these experiments a daylight lamp, D55, was used. The box was made so that the light did not leak out and affect the room situation. The observers placed colour samples in the box to be visually matched with identity colour and colour variations on the walls. They were instructed to choose the sample, or an interpolation between several samples, which they found to be the best match. Their data were noted and arranged in tables for analysis. Comparisons were made between the same *inherent colour* under likely comparable conditions in north- and south orientations. (See figure 3)

For evaluation of the experience of colour and room, some method was required. Such a method for description was developed and is called the *Associative, Reflective* method. This method originated in the will to use the means of a designer, and since the aim was to increase design knowledge it seemed useful to work with a designer's special work procedure. A designer must be attentive to appearances, enjoy focusing and testing different impacts, and be able to express these as images or characters. Theoretically, the associative, reflective method is influenced and inspired by the phenomenological theory, in approaching colours as phenomena. Colours become a phenomenon together with room and light. Through an intentional concern in experiencing phenomena in themselves, one can sense colours and the whole situation as a work of art. In describing experiences the observers wrote descriptions in their own words. In the form for notations, various aspects of colour appearance found a mean for description, including impressions of changes over time. The colour character could be described as filled, brilliant, greyish, beautiful, gloomy, glaring, dull, or hard to define. In describing the room character a semantic scale in three steps was used. Impressions of emotional tone (light- heavy), dynamism (advancing-receding), spatial quality (closed or open, distinct or diffused) and character (warm- cool) were noted.

6. RESEARCH OBSERVATIONS

6.1 Shifts in Hue and Nuance

The investigation showed distinct and settled shifts in hue and nuance between the rooms depending on their compass orientation. In sunlight all colours changed to be more chromatic, warmer and more yellowish. Greenish blue and blue colours shifted towards green. In sky- light, the inherent pale yellow colour in most cases appeared as less yellow, with either more blackness or whiteness. The blue and greenish- blue colours changed towards elementary blue, both in hue and chromaticness. Also small shifts in hue, even as small as 5 – 10 steps in the NCS scale, were noticed as distinctly different hues in the room. (See figure 4)

Reddish- blue colours could vary, as by chance, both in sunlight and sky- light. Often the inherent colour appeared as more reddish in sunlight, although in all cases the same hue was found in sky- light. It was experienced as a distinct hue shift, although we still found the colour sample among the samples picked out for the north facing room. This sort of result might have depended on a methodological problem with the colour reference box; and it is therefore my intention to make further studies on this.

6.2 Occasional Colour Variations

Occasional colour variations were often decisive for colour appearance. During the investigation it was noticed that a hue shift in the identity colour could be accounted for by different factors. Either it was an overall hue shift in colour appearance or, a hue shift could arise as a general impression from occasional colour variations. This can be related to the phenomena of assimilation, concerning how colours are affected by other colours in patterns etc. In assimilation, colours seem to blend, as opposed to contrast effects. Colour variations were often decisive for colour appearance, even when they did not show in the identity colour evaluation. For additional reasons, shadows in particular, were an issue of great importance for colour appearance. Most important, it seemed that their hue often differed from nearby areas. That implied a more complex *total appearance*.[8] In experiencing the room together with colours and light, these variations were included in a general impression. On top of this, shadow and shade contained layers of deep symbolic nature. This was significant in evaluating what the colour looked like. (See figure 5)

8. Hutchings has introduced the concept of total appearance. It involves series of images including colour. There are two classes of appearance image, the impact, or gestalt image, and the sensory, emotional and intellectual image. The total appearance treats the background to consider how people respond to images and behave. Those images are founded on both biological ground and social training and include several aspects such as security, climate, landscape, memory needs, and definitions of the object or scene.

6. 3. The Term Elasticity has been Developed

Hue shifts depending on changes in light conditions inside each room over periods of time were also observed.[9] When the sky in the north- facing room eventually became fully overcast the elementary yellow colour (S1030 -Y) turned to looking more like wet hay (greyish-brownish). As this investigation was based purely on colour appearance and therefore lacked the apparatus for measuring light levels, we did not know what exactly caused the hue shifts. Regardless of one reason or another, distinct hue shifts were observed not only between rooms but also, during the day, inside each room. As these hue shifts constantly returned, it seemed important to take them into account. In evaluating colour appearance in rooms, one single colour cannot be chosen as representative for various lighting situations in one room. Therefore, the term elasticity is defined as "the range of different colour appearances of an inherent colour inside the room."[10] From mutual experience in research, Billger and myself started to define elasticity from different lighting situations. Billger describes the term as: "the way a specific coloured material can vary in appearance under different specified conditions in a room."[11] From my viewpoint I define it as "the way a specific coloured material can vary in appearance under different periodical variations due to daylight conditions in a room". The elasticity concept can be helpful in establishing what a chosen colour might look like in a planned room. A range of colour notations likely to be seen under normal weather conditions in a room, instead of a single colour seen only occasional, would be useful in design work.

6.4 The concept of Warm and Cool Colours

The concept of warm and cool colour appearance is more complex than was expected. It was concluded that they consisted of different aspects beside hue. The first aspect was the association with warm as opposed to cool phenomena, as fire and ice. In this respect blue was always cool and red was always warm. The second

9. By atmospheric conditions there are constant changes in light level and spectral composition.
10. Hårleman, 2000. page 41.
11. Billger 1999. page 12. For instance, a specific yellow paint which is used in a room might possess an elasticity to appear greenish- yellow in a fluorescent illumination, to appear yellow but with a low degree of chromaticness in daylight, and to look strong and slightly reddish yellow in incandescent light.

aspect was the relation between other colours in comparison; because of this we could speak of "warm red" and "cool red". The third aspect was blackness and chromaticness in combination. In the investigation I found a connection between "warm" and whiteness as opposed to "cool" and blackness. Though, in some cases there was a weak connection between warm and blackness as well. A fourth aspect seemed to be "colourfulness" as opposed to "less colourful".

6.5 Advancing and Receding Colours

Some colours were advancing while others were receding. In spite of basic knowledge about the capacity of colours to advance or recede, this was a stunning experience. In sunlight most colours were advancing. However, yellow and reddish- yellow colours were most strongly advancing and seemed to fill the whole room. On those occasions, the chromaticness was highly increased and the hue shift was 5-10 steps toward red. The increased chromaticness, together with the hue shift, seemed to cause this effect, as it was not as legible for pale colours. In sky- light, yellow colours were often dull, having less chromaticness and more whitish or blackish, except for those moments when they occasionally shone up due to changes in the atmospheric conditions. They were neither advancing, nor receding. On the other hand, it was found that the reddish- blue colours were strongly receding in sky- light. Elementary blue and greenish- blue appeared as vaguely receding.

6. 6. The Room Character

Colours with high chromaticness made the room secluded and introvert. Light was seen in the landscape outside and it only shone in as a small, lustrous patch on the wall, but still did not seem to affect the room or the colours in the room. On these occasions the wall colour seemed to hold both the room and the observer as hostage; inside and not really able to take part in what was going on outside. Yellow and especially the greenish- yellow colours, were the opposite, as light made them luminous.

The south- and north- facing rooms could be characterised as having either a warm or cool character. This room character probably arose in the interaction between physical temperatures, the colour of light, emotions, and memories of the whole situation. The question of warm and cool seems to depend merely upon a mental state - and affects us differently as individuals.

7. METHODOLOGICAL DISCUSSION

The colour reference box is a helpful aid in colour matching. The method is still under development by Billger who has described some adaptation effects between artificial daylight and incandescent light. In a few extreme situations, the observers in my investigation experienced the different light situation between the room and the Colour Reference Box as a possible problem in colour matching. One situation was when the south- facing room was painted in yellow colours and the light in the Colour Reference Box looked bluish. The other was in the north- facing room with bluish colours where the light in the box looked yellowish. A preliminary test was carried out to see if we could map out the adaptation effect between the northern and southern light situation. However, we could not detect any clear tendencies for the adaptation effect in the daylight studies.[12] Figures from this investigation are not changed on account of several factors; they correspond well with verbal descriptions, memory colours and the painted pictures used in the investigation. We have to carry out more studies of this effect concerning rooms in daylight, to be ensured of this. Still, I used the method and found it reliable in my studies.

It is apparent that full-scale studies in colour research are of importance for colour research and for interior architecture. I also found it most useful with a reflective attention in describing colours and rooms, to grasp the phenomena involved. The method gave possibilities to express even unexpected experiences of colour and room character. The concept of identity colour did not work out properly in this study, probably because it does not cover the range of colour variations that are significant for these spaces. It might be useful to work out a way to catch a wider range of colour variations in the identity colour as opposed to only one notation.

12. By collaboration, adaptation effects in some situations with artificial light were mapped out; hence they can be compensated for and controlled. A preliminary curve has been worked out describing tendencies for different inherent hues in situations with artificial lighting. This way it can be made possible to foresee not only hue changes but also the approximate size of these changes.

8. CLOSING THOUGHTS

The contrasting conditions of north- and south facing rooms cause shifts in hue and nuance, but also impressions with other qualities, such as colour quality, colourfulness, room character and experienced temperature in colour. The task is to form a clear relationship between architecture, colour design and the compass orientation of interiors. Colour design would improve knowledge in making better use of colours, as well as light and shadow. Given a greater importance, colours would contribute to an extended meaning in architecture, instead of being interchangeable. It is exciting to imagine colour designs made to emphasise different locations in compass orientation. Colours that are chosen to fit the colour of light would enrich the built environment. They would clarify shades and shadows and take north- and south facing rooms into account as a rhythm in built areas.

In my investigation it became clear how colour appearance functions on several levels. For myself, as an architect and designer, the most important level is a total colour appearance. Colours are, as a part of the built environment, only momentary objects in focus. Mostly they form a background for activities in life. As an example, yellow-painted walls in a north facing room, could on a cloudy day literally be described as follows:

> Like a paper in the fireplace,
> quickly crumbling dark,
> while burning to ashes.

It now remains to deepen the questions at issue. As presented in this article, a hue shift in general has been shown concerning some yellowish and bluish colours. Green and red colours remain to be studied. For further investigations the room perspective remains to be focused upon, - that is, the character of the room painted in a specific colour. In connection with this it is important to investigate further the concept of warm and cool character. It seems to be essential to use concepts like these to grasp the experience of colour.

REFERENCES

Billger, M. *Colour in Enclosed Space. Observation of Colour Phenomena and Development of Methods for Identification of Colour Appearance in Rooms*. Chalmers, Gothenburg 1999. ISBN 91-7197-820-8.

Billger, M. *Assessing Colour Appearance in a Real Room Using Magnitude Estimation and Colour Matching Techniques*. MPL Proceedings, London April 2000.

Fridell Anter, K. *What colour is the red house? Perceived colour of painted facades*. Royal Institute of Technology, Stockholm, 2000. TRITA- ARK 2000:4. ISBN 91-7170-595-3.

Hutchins, J. *Colour in folklore*. Colour Report F50, AIC Colour and Psychology, Gothenburg 1996.

Hutchings, J. *Color in Anthropology and Folklore*, in Colour for Science, Art and Technology. Editor, Nassau, K. Elsevier 1998.

Hård, Sivik & Svedmyr. *Belysning och färgseende 2.*. Färgrapport F23, Färginstitutet, Stockholm 1983.

Hårleman, M. *Färg i norr- och södervettande rum. Kulörtonförskjutning genom varierande ljusförhållanden.* KTH, Stockholm 2000. Trita-Ark 2000:4. ISBN 91-7170-590-2.

Liljefors, A. *Lighting and Colour Terminology. Visually – Physically.* AIC Colour and Psychology, Gothenburg 1996.

Liljefors, A. *THE ViP LIGHTING THEORY- BASIC KNOWLEDGE TO LIGHTING DESIGN ON VISION AND ITS PHYSICAL STIMULUS*, p. 151. CIE proceeding - 99.

Liljefors, A. *Seende och ljusstrålning.* Baskompendium ALV Belysningslära, KTH Stockholm 1997.

Sivik, L. *Om färgers betydelse, i Upplevelser av färg och färgsatt miljö*. Byggforskningsrådet Färgantologi bok 2. 1995. ISBN 91-540-5696-9.

A bleak colour lights
giving it a warm
In the north the colour is
A kind of worthy melancholy
One wall is beige.

Light, reddish yellow (S 1010-Y20R), one big room
with daylight from both gables

the south-facing room
and soft impression.
pink – as a thin skin.
beholds the room.

ABSTRACT

This paper deals with the methodological problem of comparing colour appearance in different rooms. In order to enable comparisons that aim to map out, and describe, the elasticity in colour appearance of certain inherent colours under varying lighting conditions in rooms, a *colour reference box method* is developed. The colour reference box with its fixed illumination provides a reference situation, where colour samples can be visually matched to the colours of the room. This paper presents, and discusses this method by giving some examples from full scale room studies. It treats the specific problem of *the adaptation effect*: that is the colour sample in the colour reference box is perceived differently, as the observer adapts to various lighting conditions. For the studies presented, the way of adjusting the data in accordance to this effect is shown. In addition to the colour reference box method, visual assessments and ver-bal descriptions of the perceived colours were made.

The colour reference box is considered to solve a methodological problem. The colour reference box has also shown to be a helpful aid to visually evaluate and describe the qualitative differences in colour appearance between the *colour variations* in a room. The colour variations are considered to have great importance for the perception of the *identity colour*, and for the experience of the room.

Keywords: adaptation, colour appearance, colour difference, daylight, incandescent lamps, floures-cent lamps, interior lighting,

A Method for Comparison of Colour Appearance in Differently Illuminated Rooms

Billger, M. & Hårleman, M.

Published in CIE´s conference proceedings, publication 133, vol. 1. part. 67-71, 1999.

1. INTRODUCTION

Our research project aims at a profound understanding of colour appearance in rooms. As the lighting conditions are essential for the appearance of the room and its colours, it is important to investigate the influence of different light sources. In order to enable comparisons between perceived colours in differently illuminated rooms, a method is under development that involves a colour reference box. The colour reference box with its standard source of illumination provides a reference situation, where colour samples can be visually matched to the colours of the room. However, there is a crucial problem connected with the use of it: the colour sample in the colour reference box is perceived differently, as the observer adapts to various lighting conditions. This *adaptation effect* needs to be mapped out in order to adjust the data that are achieved, when reference samples are matched to the room colours. Our paper aims at presenting, and discussing the reliability of the colour reference box method by giving some examples from full scale room studies. The perceived colours in the rooms were identified by matching the appearance of NCS colour samples (placed in the box) to the appearance of the room surfaces. These data were adjusted in accordance to the adaptation effect between the specific light situations to compare, and thereby we could estimate the differences in colour appearance between the differently illuminated, but equally painted rooms. Finally, we compared the quantity of these differences to differences achieved by visual estimations of the perceived colours in the rooms.

2. BACKGROUND

This project is based on the design problem of predicting the outcome of a colour design. That we have variations in colour appearance due to various factors in rooms are not considered as a design problem, the problem is the lack of knowledge that can prevent us from reaching an intended result with a colour plan. We deal with colour appearance in rooms under various viewing and lighting conditions, and an important question for the project is how to identify and compare colour appearance in different rooms. Methods need to be developed for identification of perceived colours [1,2]. For a method to be practical for room studies, it should allow only one or two observers to characterise a room, and make reliable identifications of the perceived colours. Verbal descriptions are necessary but lack precision. Although, a magnitude estimation method enables a more precise location in colour space, the need of a group of well-trained observers makes it impractical for room studies. We assume that a method involving matches between reference colour samples and the perceived room colours would be ideal. However, reference colour samples requires a standard situation to be placed in, otherwise the sample will change colour appearance due to different room light. Hence, the method involving the light box was developed. A colour reference box with a fixed illumination can provide us with a standard situation for colour samples that can be matched with colours in the room, in order to identify and exemplify these colours. However, there are specific problems with this solution that has to be sorted out before such a colour reference box can be reliable. We can prevent light to shine into the eyes of the observer, and the sample in the box to be affected by the room light and the colours in the room, but we still have *the adaptation effect* to deal with. This adaptation effect is caused by the observer's adaptation to the prevailing light in the room, and makes the sample to appear differently, when the colour reference box is placed in rooms with different light situations. The adaptation effect between the light situations involved in a room comparison must be mapped out before the colour reference box can be used to identify colour appearance in the rooms.

Before applying the colour refrerence box method a validation of the box was conducted. This study [3] aimed to establish whether, or not, the adaptation effect could be mapped out, and therby possible to control. 18 observers were asked to visually assess the hue of 15-65 NCS colour samples by using a magnitude estimation method. The assessments of the samples were made in two different room lights, incandescent light and simulated daylight. The result of the study showed a clear tendency for hue differences between perceiving the same samples, placed in the light box, when being adapted to incandescent light compared to simulated daylight. It was concluded that the problem with the observer's adaptation to the room light can be described and controlled, although complementary studies are needed to quantify the differences with more accuracy, and to investigate the differences in nuance perception.

3. EXPERIMENTAL DESIGN

Examples are given from two different room studies, where the colour reference box method has been applied. In the first study, *the artificial light study*, the method was applied and evaluated in the room used for the validation of the colour reference box (referred to above). A comparison was made between the colour appearances of the walls and floor in the room illuminated with either simulated daylight, or incandescent light. The room was multi-coloured in two variations: one blue/green/grey and white, and the other violet/green/grey and white. In the other study, *the daylight study*, comparisons were made between the appearances of a room that was lighted with either direct sunlight from the south, or skylight from the north. This room was painted monochromatic in two different nuances of 3 yellow hues and 3 blue hues. Yet, we have only preliminary results of the adaptation effect between these light situations in this study. Anyway, examples from this study are included because they show other ways to analyse colour appearance with the aid of the colour reference box, then the first one.

In the studies presented, the colour appearances of the room surfaces were, first, verbally described when being adapted to each light situation. In the artifical light study, visual scaling also was used to more precisely assess the hue. The observers assessed the hue by estimating its likeness to the four elementary colours: blue, red, green and yellow, and marked the hue on an NCS hue circle. Thereafter, matches were made between samples placed in the colour reference box and the room colours. After approximately 20 minutes adaptation to the room light, different samples were placed in the colour reference box until a satisfactory match was reached. Usually no colour sample makes a perfect match to the room surface's colour appearance; an interpolation between samples is needed. It is important to look at the sample in the box for short moments; to avoid to get adapted to the light in the box instead of the light in the room. The colour reference box was placed in the middle of the room and rotated around to get a good view of the walls. In the artificial light study, only the *identity colours* were identified. The identity colour is defined as the main impression of coloured units of a room that is perceived as uniformly coloured. In the daylight study, also *colour variations* were identified. These are all the variations of the identity colour due to various viewing and lighting conditions.

4. RESULTS

4.1 Data Analysis

The data from the two room studies needs to be adjusted according to the results from colour reference box validations in the specific room lights. The data from the room studies is the NCS-codes of the samples (or the interpolation between samples) that were estimated to match colour appearance of the room surfaces. The colour qualities of these reference colour samples were analysed in accordance with the known adaptation effect to the specific light situations in the rooms. A limitation here is that we, yet, only have studied the adaptation effect for the hue. After this analysis, we got the size in NCS-steps of the perceived hue difference between the two light situations. Thirdly, to evaluate if the quantity of these differences in hue seemed to be reliable, we compared them with the visual assessments of the same room colours. For the daylight study we compared with the verbal descriptions.

4.2 Examples from the Artificial Light Study

To show how the adjustment of the data is done, two examples are given from the artificial light study. The presented results are of the difference in identity colour of one of the violet walls, and the green corner. For the room in the artificial light study, the adaptation effect had showed to have a clear tendency, when changing the room light from incandescent light to simulated daylight. The shift was towards yellow-orange with a breaking point between R90B and B. For example, the size of the difference in hue was approx. 20 NCS-steps for a B50G-sample and approx.10 steps for a R50B-sample, between the two light situations (see figure 1).

The violet wall was perceived as more red-dish in incandescent light. The sample NCS 2020-R30B was identified as the closest match. In the room with simulated daylight, an interpolation between samples gave that 2035-R65B was estimated to match. The difference in hue between these data is 35 NCS-steps. After an adjustment in accordance with the estimated adaptation effect the difference is adjusted to 20 NCS-steps (see figure 2). The green corner was perceived as more yellowish in incandescent light. The sample NCS 2050- G60Y was chosen as the closest match. In the room with simulated daylight, 2035-G15Y was estimated to match. The difference in hue between these data is 45 NCS-steps. After an adjustment in accordance with the estimated adaptation effect the difference is adjusted to 20 NCS-steps. (see figure 3). These hue differences of approximately 20 NCS-steps in both cases above, coincide with the differences between the visual assessments of the room colours.

4.3 Examples from the Daylight Study

In the validation of the colour reference box in the artificial light study, the observers perceived the light in the colour reference box as different when being adapted to the different room lights. When being adapted to incandescent light, it was lightly bluish, when being adapted to simulated daylight it was perceived as warm white. In the daylight study, the only situation, where the light in the box was perceived as distinctly chromatic, was when the room was painted reddish yellow and lighted with direct sunlight. Then the light in the box was perceived as bluish. However, even if the observers were not aware of any difference between the light in the colour reference box, when being adapted to the different daylight situations, there seems to be a difference smaller, but parallel to the one in the artificial daylight study.

Two examples from comparisons of identity colours in the daylight study are presented here. The first example deals with the room painted in NCS S1030-B, the second deals with the nuances S1010 and S1030 of Y20R. In skylight, the room painted in 1030-B was described as having a strong elementary blue colour. In sunlight, it was described as "softer" and more greenish. When analysing the identity colours, in the two light situations, with the aid of the colour reference box, samples with a difference of 10 NCS-steps in hue were chosen. We did not find any adaptation effect in hue for the B sample; no adjustments of the data were made. The identity colour was lighter and more greenish in sunlight. In skylight it was both stronger in chromaticness, and blackness.

A sample with the hue Y20R, placed in the colour reference box, was assessed to appear as more orange, when being adapted to skylight from the north. The room painted in S1010-Y20R was reddish yellow in sunlight, and pink in skylight. The room painted in S1030-Y20R was orange in skylight. In sunlight it was stronger in chromaticness, and distinctly more yellowish. In the colour reference box, however, the hue of the sample chosen to match the identity colour in the room lighted with skylight was 5 NCS-steps more yellowish, than the sample chosen to match in sunlight. However, the adaptation effect makes a Y20R-sample to appear at least 20 NCS-steps more reddish when adapted to skylight from the north, compared to being adapted to sunlight. This means that the colour reference box method gave a difference in hue that was at least 15 NCS-steps.

In addition to these comparisons between the identity colours of the room, the colour variations were analysed. For example, the colour variations of the room painted in S1030-Y20R showed very small differences in hue and chromaticness in sunlight, compared to its appearance in skylight. The shadows were more reddish when the room was lighted with skylight, and more brownish when the room was lighted with sunlight. With the aid of the colour reference box, the locations of the two extremes in hue, and the most whitish, the most chromatic, and the most blackish colour variation were defined. This information is considered to be valuable in a discussion about the relation between an identity colour and its colour variations [4], as well as for the appearance of the gestalt of the room.

5. DISCUSSION

The colour reference box is under development, and the results presented are preliminary. Much work remains in order to understand the adaptation effect in different light situations. More assessments are needed for the hue, to more accurately quantify the differences. We know that the perception of the nuance changes when the room light varies, and the difference in blackness and chromaticness needs to be investigated. The examples given above of differences in nuance between the different room lights are included to more thoroughly describe the application of the method, any conclusions of these comparisons, made with the colour reference box, cannot be drawn before the adaptation effect on chromticness and blackness is known. However, in the examples the verbal descriptions supports the shown results.

When applying the colour reference box method, there could occur a specific problem. If the light in the box is perceived as strongly chromatic, I might have to choose, what could be experienced as, extreme reference colour samples to match the room colours. E.g., one has to use blue samples with very low chromaticness to compensate for the blue light in the box. The problem is not that the adaptation effect makes one choose samples with an NCS-code that has a large difference to the perceived hue. The problem is that there are not enough NCS colour samples to cover the range of the perceived colours. When there are too few colour samples in a hue area, and it is necessary to interpolate between samples to estimate all three parameters, blackness, chromaticness and hue, the interpolation can be difficult

6. CONCLUSIONS

- The colour reference box is developed in order to enable comparisons that aim to map out, and describe, the elasticity in colour appearance of certain inherent colours under varying lighting conditions in rooms. For these comparisons of differently illuminated, but equally painted rooms, the colour reference box is considered to solve a big methodological problem.
- The colour reference box has also shown to be a helpful aid to visually evaluate and describe the qualitative differences in colour appearance between the colour variations in a room. The colour variations are considered to have great importance for the perception of the identity colour, and for the experience of the room.
- We have found magnitude estimation impractical for room studies because it requires a group of well trained observers. However, the method is considered as invaluable as an instrument to check methods under development. For example, when the colour reference method is applied, it creates a reversed way

to check and define the quantity of the adaptation effect between the different room lights. If one compares the adjusted results, achieved by doing colour matches between the colour reference box, and the colours perceived in the room, with visual assessments of the colours in the room, the adjusted results can be controlled. This control requires a study employing well trained observers that use magnitude estimation to assess the room colours.

7. REFERENCES

[1] Fridell Anter, Karin: Metoder för bestämning av uppfattad färg på fasader, Stockholm 1997.

[2] Billger, Monica: The identification of Colour in Spatial Situations, CTH Gothenburg, 1996.

[3] Billger, Monica: Comparisons of colour appearance in differently illuminated rooms. In proceedings for the conference Colour between Art and Science, Oslo, 1998

[4] Billger, Monica: Colour and Space- The identification of colour in spatial situations. In Colour Report 50, Proceeding for Colour and Psychology, intermediate AIC meeting in Göteborg 1996, ed.: Sivik Lars, Scandinavian Colour Inst.,Stockholm 1997, pp. 75-78.

ACKNOWLEDGEMENTS

This work has been supported by a grant from the Swedish Building Research Council, the Swedish Association of Painting Contractors, and the Swedish Painters Union. It has also been supported by the foundation Lars Hiertas minne.

Earnestness. As an
The light makes the colour
The inner parts of the room
as morning air

More chromatic reddish blue (S 1030-R80B) in the south

experience of presence.
quiver as nostrils.
look basement cool,
or dew on grass.

ABSTRACT

The article presents a study on colour appearance in natural daylight from different compass directions in Sweden. The intention of the study was to forecast how certain colours in the red-green sector would appear in a specific room, to help architects and designers in achieving required results from colour schemes. The problem was to find trends between inherent colour and identity colour in rooms facing different directions and illuminated by different kinds of natural light. An empirical study of dominantly reddish and greenish colours was conducted using full-scale rooms facing towards and away from the sun. Identity colours were described using five comparative methods. Results were compared with a previous study in environmental colour design concerned with yellowish and bluish colours. The study shows a regular pattern in shift of hue and nuance, from inherent colour to identity colour. In general, room identity colours were more chromatic and less whitish than inherent colours. In the room facing towards the sun all identity colours increased in chromaticness, particularly yellowish colours while reddish colours had least increase. Colours with a yellowish attribute shifted towards elementary yellow. In the room facing away from the sun a hue shift towards bluish-red was observed, and all colours increased in chromaticness, except yellowish colours.

Key words: Colour appearance, coloured walls, full-scale room, natural daylight, sunlight and skylight, inherent colour, identity colour, environmental colour design.

Study of Colour Shifts in Various Daylights: Dominantly Reddish and Greenish Rooms Illuminated by Sunlight and Skylight

Hårleman, M.

Submitted to: Colour: Design and Creativity May 31, 2006.

Accepted for publication Jan 10, 2007.

1. INTRODUCTION

Choosing colours for interior design purposes poses the difficulty of trying to foresee how a planned design will appear in a given room. There is a general awareness that differences between a chosen colour sample and the end result can be expected. This is often encountered with the colour on room walls, which can differ quite markedly from that of the chosen colour sample. Colour appearance will also vary in rooms facing in different compass directions, i.e. rooms illuminated with different qualities of daylight. There are many different causes: visual, physical, psychological and emotional. The point of departure is those perceptual differences arising from rooms facing different compass directions, i.e. differences that endure after light adaptation. While much research has been conducted charting changes experienced in the colour of flat surfaces, colour appearance in three-dimensional space is a relatively new field. In recent years, Billger has worked with full-scale studies of rooms in artificial light, showing how lighting causes different patterns of colour appearance [1-4].

The present study was carried out between 0900 hours and 1500 hours during long summer days in Stockholm, Sweden. North- and south-facing rooms were chosen, since light conditions diverge the most between these two directions; the north-facing room was illuminated by skylight and the south- facing by sunlight. The intention was to gain an understanding regarding how such variations might appear for daylight-illuminated rooms with systematically selected inherent colours, since such an understanding is hitherto lacking. The aim was to conduct a systematic charting of any colour shifts from the chosen colour sample to the colour appearance in the room.

Empirical studies were conducted to investigate and map the nature of colour shift patterns. Comparative methods with colour matching, memory matching and verbal description were used and further developed in full-scale studies in daylight. Twelve hues in two nuances were chosen from the NCS colour circle, with a perceptually equal distance between the chosen hues. The walls in two full-scale rooms were painted one at a time with these inherent colours.

This survey is part of a larger project relevant to colouring of interiors in daylight, and will be applicable to all such circumstances. The project was carried out in two phases with the same nuances but different hues. A similar study concentrating on yellowish and bluish colours has been published previously [5-6]. The current article focuses on reddish and greenish colours, and consequently is referred to as the 'red-green study'. Reddish colours are referred to in terms of 'pinkish', since reddish colours in these nuances generally are called pink. A part study is previously presented [7].

1.1 Terminology

The NCS (natural colour system) was used and its colour terminology was adopted [8]. Thus *colour* is defined as 'that which human beings see as colour as used to define objects and background on the basis of colour differences'. *Hues* are defined according to their relation to the six elementary colours red, blue, green, yellow, black and white. Hue relation is shown through its position in the colour circle. Thus orange has two *chromatic elementary attributes*: yellow and red. The colour triangle shows the colour *nuance*, described in visual proportions of blackness, whiteness, and *chromaticness*. Chromaticness is the sum of a colour's chromatic attributes.

Colour appearance is used as a general concept for research concerning how coloured materials appear under different lighting and viewing conditions[1]. The term *inherent colour* is used to denote the colour an object would have if observed in

1. The ASTM standard defines terms used in description of *appearance* includes, but are not limited to colour, gloss, opacity, scattering, texture, and visibility of materials and light sources.

standard observation conditions used where the NCS colour samples accord with their colour notation[2]. The term *perceived colour* emphasises the importance of subject and colour changeability. I have, however, chosen to consistently use the term identity colour, which has evolved for colour studies in three-dimensional space [1, p 11]. *Identity colour* is defined as the main colour impression of surfaces or parts of a room that are perceived to be uniformly coloured. Local colour appearances, called colour variations, might depend on light distribution, reflections from other surfaces and contrast effects. The identity colour is a term corresponding to a holistic attitude, using real rooms instead of experimental set-ups. As a specific coloured material can vary in appearance under different specified conditions in a room, that phenomenon is called *colour elasticity.* This elasticity can be shown as an extension in three dimensions in colour space, or as mapped-out areas in the NCS colour circle and the colour triangle. [1, p12]

The difference between inherent and identity colours I term *shift*. This shift is described as the difference between inherent and identity colour expressed as steps in the NCS colour circle and colour triangle. I distinguish between a *hue shift, nuance shift* and *colour shift*, the latter being a shift in both hue and nuance. The *breaking point* [3] is a specified point in colour space where a general trend in shift stops and is replaced by a trend in another direction [9].

I use light quality referring to differences in daylight indoors due to compass direction. Natural daylight contains variations in spectral characteristic, light distribution and luminous intensity. These variations cause differences in spatial- and colour perception. Thus colour impressions in a room can change, both in hue and nuance. The perceived colour of light is a quality in daylight as well as in artificial light. Light itself has no intrinsic colour, but in rooms with a corresponding inherent colour it can appear to have its own colour. Sunlight can be said the have a light colour, which amplifies yellow elementary qualities, something that skylight usually, does not do [10-11].

2. A D65 light source is used in the NCS standard situation compared to natural daylight used in this study.
3. Fridell Anter has previously used breaking point to denote a specified point in colour space where the general shift tendency discontinues and the inherent colour and perceived colour coincide. I use identity colour where Fridell Anter uses the term perceived colour.

1.2 Research on Colour Coordinates in Daylight

There is a gap between different disciplines in colour research. Such a gap exists between the discipline on colour coordinates and environmental studies. The latter discipline is uncertain on result usability in connection to ordinary life outside the laboratory. Despite knowledge of some, so called effects, it is still unknown how they might affect colour in environmental situations.

It is well known [12, p 79] that the intensity of illumination cause changes in perceived colour. At low luminance levels, red and green hues predominate over yellow and blue. The reverse is true at high luminance (the Bezold-Brücke effect). Increasing the intensity of coloured lights causes colours with a wavelength greater than 505 nm to shift towards yellow; those with wavelengths shorter than 505 nm shift toward blue. Three particular wavelengths are found to be invariant, purest blue (470 nm), green (505 nm), and yellow (572 nm). Increases in light intensity are also found to produce increases in saturation (the Abney effect). Unsaturated blues and reds shift toward purple (Burns et al 1984).

In 2002, Romero *et al.* published a study concerning colorimetric changes on objects illuminated by natural daylight in Granada, Spain [13, p. 27]. The horizontal surfaces of objects were measured at different solar elevations, on separate days, in different seasons, and under diverse meteorological conditions. The aim was to measure trends in daylight-correlated colour temperature, but not in relation to luminance. Comparisons were made between different solar elevations during the day, and between different days. Most important was that variations in the chromaticity coordinates followed the tendency shown by daylight itself. They elucidate the results as follows: *If we express this in terms of appearance, the trends would be to diminish or to augment the red content respectively. Another way to express this would be that the variations are given in the red-green direction, depending on the relative yellow-blue content in the object's color.*

1.3 Research on Environmental Colour

In 1983 Hård *et al.* conducted a study comparing colour samples in different types of lighting [14]. This was based on the fact that the sides of objects, when illuminated by different light sources, such as fluorescent or incandescent lighting, will have different colours. The study showed that within individual parts of the colour realm, varied illumination resulted in varying degrees of shift both in nuance and hue. Nuance shifts were small for slightly chromatic colours, but the more chromatic had a clear tendency towards greater chromaticness, except for blue where chosen samples were markedly blacker. From standard light (daylight fluorescent 5400 K) to incandescent light, yellow-green inherent colour gave a colour shift towards green; green to blue-green, blue-green to blue, and certain of the bluish inherent colours gave a colour shift to greater blueness. Yellow inherent colours gave a colour shift towards yellow-red, yellow-red to red, blue-red to blue; while red inherent colours displayed only minor hue shifts, most often towards yellow-red.

Billger conducted experiments with model and full-scale rooms, comparing colours in two- and three-dimensional studies [1-2]. I used Billger's methods and the term *identity colour* for colour studies in rooms. Billger developed a colour reference box for use in colour magnitude estimation [3-4]. The colour reference box enables comparison between identity colours in a room and colour samples placed in the box. The latter are illuminated with one form of artificial light source, artificial daylight (5400 K) and incandescent light (2800K), while the room is illuminated with a different type. With these experiments, Billger could show evidence of patterns in colour variation. Test sequences concerning the colour reference box showed different scales, and could be constructed depending on different combinations of artificial lighting in both room and box. Identity colour was experienced as moving around the colour circle in different directions, depending on source of illumination. Yet all colour samples in the box were perceived as more yellowish in the room with simulated daylight compared with the room lit by incandescent illumination, regardless of the light source in the box. Hue shift tendencies valid for incandescent light and simulated daylight seemed to be comparable with results from my own daylight study of yellowish and bluish colours in rooms in sunlight and skylight respectively. Hue shift tendencies for colours in incandescent light are similar to tendencies in sunlight, and hue shift tendencies for simulated daylight are similar to tendencies in skylight.

Fridell Anter conducted colour studies in daylight to examine differences between inherent and perceived colours of facades [9]. Various types of lighting such as skylight and sunlight made up the variables, along with angle of observation, distance of observation and adjoining colours. She established that the difference between inherent and perceived colour was always greater than change caused by the different variables. Perceived colour always differed from inherent colour in nuance and sometimes in hue, the main difference being that perceived colour was always less blackish than inherent colour. Reduced blackness was compensated by greater whiteness and/or chromaticness. Whitish inherent colours resulted mostly in perceived colours in greater whiteness and unchanged chromaticness. Inherent colours with only a small proportion of whiteness increased in chromaticness, with unchanged whiteness. For hue changes she established a pattern similar to Billger's directions for colour samples in the colour reference box. Fridell Anter found that perceived hue tended in two directions from a stable position at Y50R where inherent colour and perceived colour coincide. She located a breaking point at Y45R from where hues tended anticlockwise towards another breaking point near R80B. From Y50R, colours tended in a clockwise direction towards R80B. This was most clear for more whitish nuances. Within the blue area, a zone exists between R70B and B with overlapping breaking points. Blue inherent colours with a small proportion of redness tended towards greater redness, while bluish-red inherent colours tended towards greater blueness. Light blue inherent colours tended towards blue-green, and Fridell Anter concluded that different nuances might have their own breaking points.

Hårleman's previous yellow-blue study showed that daylight variations caused two different patterns for colour appearance in rooms [5–6]. Colour shifts resulting from light from different compass directions demonstrate a pattern *between* rooms. Beside this, a pattern was found for rapid variations *within* rooms. Reflections and changes in light quality caused shifts in identity colour in two ways: by shifts in hue and nuance. Sunlight caused yellowish rooms to show increased yellowness through hue shifts towards elementary yellow. All identity colours increased in chromaticness in rooms illuminated by sunlight, but mostly the yellowish colours. In sunlight, no or only very small hue shifts were observed in rooms painted elementary yellow and elementary blue inherent colours. On the other hand, colours with two chromatic elementary attributes showed a considerable hue shift towards yellow or blue respectively. Rooms illuminated by skylight showed increased blueness (increased chromaticness with bluish colours and decreased chromaticness with yellowish colours), and hue shifts towards elementary blue (figure 1).

1.4 Problems and Objectives

One problem is to identify how the colour appearance of a given room with walls of a specific colour will be affected in terms of hue and nuance; relevant factors include room size and distance apart of coloured (vertical) walls, reflectance and uneven light distribution from a window as well as a personal interpretation of the situation. A verbal description of the room and its colour completes the illustration. Another problem is to locate how the specific light qualities will affect hue and nuance in making comparisons between the rooms. The identity colour of the room can be described with a colour matching method and a colour reference box [4]. It is important to be able to identify tendencies for any shift in hue or nuance and locate breaking points where such tendencies turn in one or another direction. The overall objective has been to acquire knowledge to facilitate a preliminary forecast, in NCS steps, of how a planned colour will appear in a given room. A normal daylight situation is taken as the norm, as colour appearance in north- and south-facing rooms usually differs over the time span 0900 to 1500 hours. Ordinary paint and colours were used, with relatively small differences in hue and nuance between inherent colours. Treatment in the present article will be confined to colour shifts and breaking points between rooms and not within them.

Will light quality cause a nuance shift also with rooms in reddish and greenish colours? Can breaking points be identified through collating study results between this study and the previous yellow-blue study? Based on previous studies, the hypothesis is that rooms in reddish and greenish inherent colours will exhibit similar hue shifts as yellowish and bluish rooms did, as follows:

1. Room walls will reflect colours towards a shift in hue and nuance
2. A room in reddish and greenish inherent colours illuminated by sunlight will increase in yellowish attributes compared with the inherent colour
3. A room lit by skylight will increase in blueness, compared with the inherent colour, implying tendencies for hue shift exist also for reddish and greenish

identity colours

4. Yellow and blue attributes will increase more in chromaticness than the reddish and greenish inherent colours.

2 STUDY DESIGN

2.1 Experimental Rooms and Observers

Two similar full-scale rooms were set up in a construction cabin positioned facing north–south. Colour temperature on a fairly cloudy day was approximately 8000 K in the northfacing and to 7000 K in the south facing room. Both rooms had similar short-end windows facing respectively north- south, and the room light was transmitted from clear, double-glazing. The cabin was placed in a slope, with vegetation in front of the room in sunlight and other houses with yellow plaster outside the room in skylight. Room measurements were 4.2 × 2.9 m. The inner surface of the walls consisted of plywood roller-painted with a new inherent colour for each test sequence. Floors were covered with beige-speckled lino, windows had white-painted frames and inner reveals and ceilings consisted of white-painted roof boarding (figure 2).

The experimental period was June to September in Stockholm, where the sun rises between 0334 and 0634 hours and sets between 2205 and 1845. In total, 72 observers made 118 observations. Observers were architects and interior designers, plus students reading these subjects. This choice of professional category, with people interested in both colour and space, was made so as to obtain, as far as possible, informed and detailed descriptions. Each observer gave two complete descriptions of colour appearance, one in each room. These together took over one hour.

2.2 Colour Selection

The colours chosen were three reddish and three greenish hues in two nuances commonly used in interior colour plans. They were chosen to have equal perceptual difference in hue between each colour sequence[4]. The nuances were whitish 1010

4. In the NCS colour system colours are arranged according to similarity with the elementary colours: white, black, yellow, red, blue and green. As a consequence, the NCS system does not define equal distance between elementary colours, and the colour circle has in fact less perceptual difference between colours in the

and the more chromatic 1030. The hues were yellowish-red (Y80R), red (R), bluish-red (R20B), bluish-green (B70G), green (G) and yellowish-green (G20Y). Due to unsuitable weather conditions over a lengthy period, one of the 12 inherent colours was omitted: the pale yellowish green colour (1010-G20Y) was left out in favour of the more chromatic yellowish green colour (1030-G20Y). One yellowish and one bluish inherent colour that were used previously and might represent possible points for hue shift were included. These hues, reddish yellow (1030-Y20R) and reddish blue (1030-R80B), showed interesting patterns of hue shift, and were therefore subjected to further study. The identity colours of inherent colours displayed different tendencies in the experimental rooms, suggesting the presence of breaking points. They can furthermore function as colour references between the two studies (figure 3).

2.3 Empirical Methods

The operative terms of the study are inherent colour and identity colour. Five methods of comparison were used:

1. Colour matching method aided by colour reference box
2. Verbal description in standardised colour terms
3. Verbal description using own vocabulary
4. Memory matching in comparison between rooms
5. Colour matching with given colour samples.

Observers remained in each experimental room throughout the individual case. After adaptation to room light conditions, perceived colour in the room was to be described verbally. A spontaneous impression of entire room would be described using the observer's own words to capture the moment, with a description relating to hue and nuance ensuing. Identifications of colour on three of the room walls were then evaluated. On the instructions of the observer, the experiment supervisor picked out colour samples to be placed in a colour reference box. The observer compared the identity colour of the room walls with colour samples in the colour reference box until a good matching was found. After that, a verbal comparison was made using the

blue-green quadrant than in the others. Consequently, I have chosen to adjust that situation by selecting one green inherent colour at a larger distance from the elementary green.

observer's own words to compare the identity colour of the wall in the current room with the colour recollected from the previous room. After completion of this series, the box was moved to the second room and the process was repeated. Finally, colour matching of both rooms with given colour samples was undertaken.

Colour Reference Box: This was the basic method for colour matching. The observers described the wall colours by comparison with colour samples placed in the box and displayed through a small opening so that the box illumination would not leak out. The samples were illuminated with a D55 light source (Osram Dulux 5500 K, R_a 96), the same in both rooms, and thus functioning as standard lighting.

Verbal Description in Standardised Colour Terms: Observers were asked to describe the identity colour's hue and nuance in terms such as reddish, yellowish, greenish, bluish, blackish, greyish and whitish. This method was used as a supplement to colour matching and has previously been used as a method of analysis.

Verbal Description with Own Vocabulary: The idea was to find means to describe colour appearance using the observers' own vocabulary of colour response in each room. A method for free mode of expression was used here in order to capture spontaneous descriptions of colour response. Colours make an instant impression that takes some time for a subject to transform into colour terms and colour codes. This first impression may persist in situations where no further description is asked for; such is the case in daily life. Therefore comparing such spontaneous descriptions with colour shift data is useful.

Memory Matching Method: This method was used for direct comparison between the rooms. Observers were asked to provide a verbal description of how the present room looked in comparison with the previous one. Comparison between the rooms was made in the second room, 20-25 min after leaving the first one. This method is concerned with the observer's instant colour impression.

Method with Given Colour Samples: This study was conducted between the two rooms. Selected colour samples were compared side by side in front of the dividing wall between rooms to achieve similar illumination on the colour samples. These samples were chosen in advance once a tendency had become clear after the initial observations, and were presented to observers as the concluding element following studies in the two rooms. A new set of colour samples was selected prior to each new inherent colour. One colour sample was chosen to represent identity colour in each room. Each set of colour samples had the same nuance, i.e. 10 steps more chromatic than the inherent colour. Hues were chosen so that the inherent colour would flank a colour sample on each side of the hue circle, along with an additional colour sample with a probable shift tendency.[5] This method was introduced to give the study greater comparative qualities. Colour matching using given colour samples is a relative and comparative method.

2.4 Methods of Analysis

Data from colour matching with the colour reference box were tabulated. Inherent colours represented points of reference, while shift was calculated as the difference between inherent and identity colours. Blackness, whiteness, chromaticness and hue of inherent and identity colours were added to the statistics, together with compass direction, weather and time data. Data were statistically analysed by simple frequency analysis as mean values. Data from the other methods described above were used for supplementary and comparative analysis, especially in cases when colour matching with the colour reference box failed to concur with the general tendency.

The box was used principally as a standard method to gain instant and comparative data, in individual cases and between cases.

3. STUDY RESULTS

Results of the study show that daylight in both rooms caused clear patterns of shift in hue and nuance, from inherent colour to identity colour; the pattern differed between compass directions, and between hues and nuance series.

Differences in nuance were recorded within the room in itself. Room identity colours had a lesser proportion of whiteness than inherent colours, in general by 10 NCS steps. There was also a clear perceptual difference in chromaticness between inherent and identity colours. Reduced whiteness was compensated for by greater chromaticness and sometimes also in blackness. The average increase in chromat-

5. When the inherent colour was 1030-R, I selected 1040-Y90R, 1040-R, 1040-R10B and 1040-R20B as given colour samples.

icness was five to 10 steps, and increase in blackness was up to five steps.

Both series of *nuances* had their own variations. The whitish nuance 1010 shifted more in hue than the 1030 nuance did. The more chromatic nuance in turn, 1030, became more chromatic. The various *hues* had individual patterns for chromaticness. This was most evident in the 1030 nuance since this series contained three more experimental colours. Chromatic patterns were heavily influenced by room compass direction. Chromatic differences were greatest with the bluish and yellowish identity colours. In most cases when the room was given the inherent colour bluish pink (1010-R20B and 1030-R20B) the study was conducted in rainy weather as can be seen from the results where these identity colours include a great deal of blackness.

3.1 Influence of Compass Direction

Hue shift tendencies were strongly influenced by the different light quality in the compass directions. The greatest chromatic increase in the reddish-blue colour (1030-R80B) was observed in the room in skylight, by 15 steps. Pinkish (1030-R), and bluish-pink (1030-R20B), greenish (1030-G), and bluish-green (1030-B70G), increased by approx. 10 steps each in chromaticness. Yellowish colours and attributes increased least in chromaticness; yellowish-green (1030-G20Y) and reddish-yellow (1030-Y20R) by only 5-6 steps, while increasing in blackness (figure 4).

The same north-facing room caused a hue shift towards a bluish hue. The greatest hue shift was caused in the whitish nuance, 1010; light bluish-green (1010-B70G) and light green (1010-G), 35 steps, the light pink (1010-R) and light bluish-pink (1010-R20B), 15-18 steps. Colours with a yellowish attribute tended towards red or green, indicating a breaking point at yellow (Y). The reddish-yellow colour (1030-Y20R) appeared as pink, and the yellowish-green (1030-G20Y) room tended towards increased greenness. Another breaking point zone was located between reddish blue and bluish red (1030-R80B and 1030-R20B). In the 1010 nuance the yellowish breaking point seems to be much closer to elementary red, between yellowish pink and pink (Y80R – R).

The greatest chromatic increase in colours with a yellowish attribute was observed in the room in sunlight; the reddish-yellow colour (1030-Y20R) used for reference purpose increased 20 steps in chromaticness, yellowish-green (1030-

G20Y) and yellowish-pink (1030-Y80R), 13 steps. The smallest increase in chromaticness, 6-7 steps, was observed with the inherent colours pink (1030-R) and bluish-pink (1030-R20B). In the same room less blackish increase in identity colours were observed in comparison with the north-facing room (figure 5). In the south-facing room, yellowish attributes tended between a stable position and a more yellowish hue. The yellowish-green room (1030-G20Y) appeared stable in hue, 0 steps, while the yellowish-pink room (1030-Y80R) tended towards elementary red, 5 steps. The reddish-yellow colour (1030-Y20R) tended towards elementary yellow, 5 steps. Remaining pinkish and greenish inherent colours shifted towards increased bluishness in both rooms, yet with fewer steps in the room facing towards the sun (figure 6). The relative difference between the north- and south facing rooms is clear (figure 7).

3.2 Colour Response with own Words

Observers applied different verbal descriptions using their own words, mostly expressions of sense data. The expressions are easy to understand but more difficult to comprehend in relation to the colour shifts. The identity colour of inherent colour 1030-Y80R in the room in skylight was described as 'sharper', and in sunlight as 'softer'. No specific data difference explaining choice of words could be found, yet the choice is so apt; there are no other differences than absence or presence of yellowness. Words such as 'soft' and 'rich' were often particularly used to describe identity colours in rooms in sunlight. In skylight, identity colours could be described as thin. Rooms in sunlight showed increased yellowness, especially pinkish colours but also greenish ones, giving a soft and rich appearance. The same inherent colours in the room illuminated by skylight seemed to lack an intermediate colour, and gave an empty, thin or sharp impression. Bluish-pink in the room facing towards the sun appeared as 'soft' when described as greyish-pink or greyish-purple, while the same inherent colour in the room facing away from the sun was described as 'horrible red' as it appeared as reddish-violet (figures 8 and 9).

4 DISCUSSION

4.1 Study Comparisons

Tendencies for hue shift from inherent colour to identity colour are the same in both interior studies. Skylight increased bluishness, likewise, sunlight enhanced yellowness in both hue and nuance. Hue shift in the north facing room tended in two directions; from yellowish towards a bluish and reddish hue. The south facing room caused the opposite tendency; from bluish and reddish inherent hue towards elementary yellow. In both cases yellowish chromaticness and a zone in the reddish blue and bluish red area, are crucial. In the previous yellow-blue study the reddish blue reference colour (1030-R80B) was unstable, but in the current a tendency towards elementary blue in the room facing towards the sun was unequivocal. The identity colour tended towards reduced redness (R90B), while the skylight caused an increased redness (R75B). This correlate well with Fridell Anters *overlapping breaking points* [9, p.107] in the blue area, between R70B and B. Blue inherent colours with a small proportion of redness tended towards greater redness, while bluish-red inherent colours tended towards greater blueness. This may depend on *the purple gap;* as the inherent colours are bluish red and reddish blue, very small changes in the light situation may cause apt colour shifts in this area.

Fridell Anter agrees on the observation that the different nuances appear to possess different breaking points. Nuance 1030 increased in chromaticness both on facades [9, p. 226], and in rooms.

4.2 Hue Shift as Perception and Response

In both rooms green inherent colours in nuance 1010 entailed the greatest hue shift, calculated in terms of number of steps in the NCS systems. Despite this, pink colours, which typically made deep emotional impacts, appeared as varying most in hue. This was noticeable in both verbal descriptions and spontaneous judgements. Might the green hue shift have been exaggerated in order to make visible the relatively small differences between hues in the green-blue sector? The distance between elementary colours in the NCS colour circle grants a perceptually greater space in the quadrant between blue and green elementary colours, i.e. small differences between hues. With the other quadrants, perceptual space is less and the difference between the various hues greater. This is particularly the case for the quadrant between red and blue. Five steps in the red-blue quadrant result in a large perceptual difference between hues, whereas five steps in the blue-green quadrant convey only a small difference. This means that the many steps in the green quadrant do not necessarily result in a major difference between hues.

Shifts in hue and nuance, even small ones, can cause major differences in colour appearance. For example, a yellowish colour, when it shifts five steps more blackish, appears as a brownish nuance; a pinkish colour, when it shows a 10 step increase in chromaticness along with a 15 step hue shift towards blue, differs clearly from the same inherent colour that undergoes a 5 step increase in chromaticness and a 5 step hue shift. Figures 9 and 10 show approximately how certain colour shifts might appear, in the relationship between rooms and between inherent colour and identity colour, despite the significant risk of erroneous colour rendition.

4.3 Discussion of Methods

Most important concerning methods in the project is the broad methodology. As these rooms were enhanced and reduced by shifts in both hue and nuance the responses are multiple.

Colour matching using the colour reference box is an effective method; through careful observation it allows observers to see the results of their matching. When an observer had difficulty in verbalise differences between hue and chromaticness, the method served to clarify, providing visible results to adjustments made. This in turn had a positive effect on verbal description. Earlier tests have shown that adaptation effects cause by the colour reference box can be calculated and corrected although adaptation showed to be negligible for the rooms in daylight [3–4]. The risk of adaptation effects for reddish and greenish inherent colours was not considered to arise, as inherent colour and light quality together do not cause maximum colour effect. Neither the supplementary analysis, nor the observer's spontaneous reactions indicated any adaptation effects though such effects cannot be completely excluded.

The new method involving given colour samples was a successful supplementary method. It lacked precision but made comparison between rooms clearer. Data from the memory matching method were used only in a supplementary analysis in cases were the observers had trouble using the colour vocabulary and that it affected the colour matching. Concerning the method involving verbal description with the observer's own vocabulary, i.e. without preconceived colour terms, it is clear that important possibilities exist here which cannot be encapsulated by official colour terminology. This was particularly clear in comparative descriptions of identity colours. Details covered by these descriptions could not be explained by any other method and they deserve to be further studied.

The hue shift tendency with natural daylight quality in the south facing room was surprising and worth another study. It was directed towards elementary yellow in two directions from areas where the yellowish attribute was weak; in the yellowish-red and the yellowish-green quadrants, respectively. The yellowish-red area corresponds with other research concerning artificial light [1, p. 18, 2] and natural daylight [9, p. 107], and the yellowish green inherent colour and identity colour coincided. This may be explained by Romero's observation [13] that an objects relative yellow-blue content show as variations also in the red-green direction.

5. CONCLUSIONS

Collating data from both interior studies a regular and considerable pattern was demonstrated for shifts in hue and nuance depending on the light quality. Sunlight, yellowish and greenish colours were concurrent as were skylight, bluish and reddish colours. Even as small changes as 3-5 NCS steps, are clearly noticeable colour shifts.

Two breaking points in hue shift directions have been identified in the north-facing room. A more complex pattern for breaking points was observed in the south-facing room.

In terms of observed nuance shifts, the room identity colours became less whitish and more chromatic compared with the inherent colour. Comparing nuances, the less chromatic nuance (1010) was associated with greater hue shifts, while the more chromatic nuance (1030) was linked to greater increases in chromaticness.

The strategy of adopting multiple methods to describe colour appearance showed considerable scope as it enables more than one aspect of colour to be registered. The technique of encouraging users to describe colours verbal using their own vocabulary seems to be a promising method for further explorations of colour appearance.

Using the colour reference box in a colour matching method, subjects were able to describe identity colour and compare colour appearance between rooms. This enabled a fine gradation between different identity colours to be made. This gradation also helps to consider colour elasticity in various cases.

6. REFERENCES

[1] M Billger, *Colour in Enclosed Space*. Gothenburg, Chalmers University of Technology, Form och Teknik. ISBN 91-7197-820-8. (1999)

[2] M Billger, Col. Res. Appl., 24 (1999) 230-242.

[3] M Billger, Col. Res. Appl., 25 (3) (2000) 214-225. Online

[4] M Billger and M Hårleman, Proc. CIE, Warsaw 1999; (CIE publication 133, Vol. 1, Part 1) 67-71.

[5] M Hårleman, *Färg i norr- och södervettande rum. Kulörtonförskjutning genom varierande ljusförhållanden*. Stockholm, Royal institute of Technology (KTH), School of Architecture (2000) ISBN 91-7170-590-2. In Swedish.

[6] M Hårleman, *Nordic Journal of Architectural Research*, 2 (2001) 41-48.

[7] M Hårleman, Proc. 9th congress, Int. Colour Assoc., Rochester, USA (SPIE, 4421 (2001) 69-71). Online

[8] A Hård and L Sivik, Col. Res. Appl., 6 (3) (1981) 129-138.

[9] K Fridell Anter, *What colour is the red house*? Perceived colour of painted façades. Stockholm, Royal Institute of Technology (KTH), School of Architecture. Academic Diss. ISBN 91-7170-595-3 (2000)

[10] A Liljefors and P Sällström, *Ljusfärg som belysningskvalitet*. Stockholm, Statens råd för byggnadsforskning, Rapport R 146 (1979) ISBN 91-540-3143-5. In Swedish.

[11] A Liljefors, "Space, glass, light" in exhibition catalogue: *Rummet på rymmen*, Stockholm, The Swedish Museum of Architecture, ISBN 91-85460-60-5, (1999) 34-47.

[12] J. Davidoff, *Cognition through Color*. The MIT Press, A Bradford Book, Cambridge, Massachusetts, London, England.

[13] J Romero, J Hernandez-Andrés, J L Nieves and J A Garcia. Col. Res. Appl., 28 (1) (2003) 25-35. Online

[14] A Hård, L Sivik and Å Svedmyr, *Belysning och färgseende* II. Undersökning av färgade föremåls olika färg under tre vanligen förekommande ljuskällor. Stockholm, Färginstitutet. Färgrapport F23, ISSN 0280-2198 (1983) 11-17. In Swedish.

Brilliant deep golden yellow. golden sparkle. A majesty that ugly, brownish shadows It darkens to brown orange shades as decaying spots ceiling. By then it mostly

More chromatic yellow (S 1030-Y) in the south

In sun as an extravagant – needing plenty of space so can be avoided. but then there are greenish from angles near floor and resembles old brass.

ABSTRACT

The perception of room character attributable to colour appearance and spatial evaluation in different compass orientations has been studied. Rooms of the same colour, but observed in light from different compass directions will appear differently, in particular their identity colours will differ.

A study is carried out in Sweden in two identical rooms, north- and south-facing. Seventy-two subjects evaluated and compared the experimental rooms. The inherent colours were six pinkish and five greenish colours, all except one in two nuances, plus one yellowish and one bluish colour, in total 13 colours. Description of room character was aided by semantic scales. Data were statistically processed using the Statistical Package for the Social Sciences (SPSS) program to analyse connections between spatial evaluation, inherent colour and compass orientation. The NCS colour vocabulary was also used. Finally, verbal descriptions using the subjects own words were used as a supplementary method to unfold nuances in response.

The study showed that differences in hue and nuance affected evaluation of room character. Subjects reacted differently in pinkish and greenish rooms, describing distinct colour connotations. Differences in direction of illumination caused weakening or strengthening of associations linked to the colours by colour connotations.

Significance of Colour on Room Character: Study on Dominantly Reddish and Greenish Colours in North- and South- Facing Rooms

Maud Hårleman*, Inga-Britt Werner* and Monica Billger†.

***School of Architecture and Built Environment,**

Royal Institute of Technology, 100 44 Stockholm, Sweden

†School of Architecture, Chalmers University of Technology, Sweden

maud@arch.kth.se, ingabritt@infra.kth.se, mpb@chalmers.se

Submitted to Colour: Design and Creativity February 2, 2007.

Accepted for publication June 4, 2007.

1. INTRODUCTION

Identically coloured rooms illuminated by light from different compass directions will not appear the same in the Nordic countries. In clear weather a south-facing room is dominated by sunlight while a north-facing room is illuminated by skylight and reflected light. As sunlight and skylight differ in luminous intensity, light direction and spectral characteristics result is a major difference in light quality. Consequently colour appearance differs between rooms even when they have been painted in the same colour, with the same paint. Traditionally these different light qualities are referred to as warm light and cold light. How does this affect evaluation of room and colour? Investigations into the effect of daylight on colour and spatial evaluation have been lacking. In teaching colour design, it is important to consider emotional response to these situations and to map out impressions of colour appearance and colour design in different daylight qualities.

This study relates to research on environmental colour design, concerning the relationship between man, environment and colour. Our aim has been to understand connections between visual appearance and the significance of light and colour on room character. The main focus of the work has examined room characters as a function of direction of illumination. What happens when rooms of the same inherent colour gain different identity colours due to light from different compass orientations? Chiefly reddish and greenish colours have been used, together with one yellowish and one bluish reference. We have evaluated space and room character. The questions to be answered are:

1. If and in what way does a room colouring affect evaluation of room character?
2. If and in what way do different daylight qualities affect room character?

The main aim has been to investigate the connection between verbal expression and emotional impression of room colours due to different light qualities. A secondary aim has been to supply and test two new meaning variables: embracing and elevating. The study is named the 'red-green study', yet the reddish colours are referred to in terms of 'pinkish', since reddish colours in the nuances used are generally called pink.

2 BACKGROUND

2.1 Different Approaches to Colour

Osgood *et al.* introduced a psychometric technique with semantic differentials used with factor analysis [1]. In this technique, subjects mark a representative value for evaluation with the help of variables or *items* on a graded scale. The problem was to find appropriate items for the study in hand. They found that items could be grouped into *factors* and showed that three mutually independent factors represented the basis of most descriptive words; these were value, activity and potency. Research concerning a subject's emotional reactions on colour, *colour emotion,* has a long history, especially among psychologists. Most studies on colour emotion have been made for single-colours or two-colour combinations [2-6].

Küller developed a method for measuring and describing evaluation of built environment, the SMB method [7]. He found eight factors: affection, complexity, enclosedness, potency, pleasantness, unity, social status and originality. Küller himself particularly pointed out affection, complexity and enclosedness as important contributors to research on spatial evaluation. Hogg *et al.* worked with simulated interiors and found five factors for colour in spatial models: dynamism, spatial quality, emotional tone, complexity and evaluation [8]. Over the years, many researchers have looked at factors influencing colour emotion [9-17]. It was concluded that items can be classified under different factors in different areas of research, for example isolated colours, colour combinations, colour in spatial models and colour on exteriors. However, concerning interior spaces, the *value factor* and a factor for *activity* and *potency* were still consistently featured in most collations of factors encountered.

2.2 Connection between Items and Factors

Many studies dealt with colour and *temperature*. Using colour samples it was found that a subject's reaction on colour is rooted in an experience of warm and cold colours [3,5]. Warmest are red, (red, orange and yellow) and coldest are blue and green, (blue and blue-green). In full-scale experiments it was found that colours do not cause an experience of a physical temperature, but can instead cause a cognitive experience with associations of warmth and coldness [8,11-13].

Küller searched for but found no simple connection between the *pleasantness* factor concerning hue and nuance [11]. Greater differences were found between nuances within each hue than between different hues. Thus there was not a straightforward connection between nuance and pleasantness, and individuals evaluated the pleasantness factor with great differences. It was found that light and whitish spaces contribute to a sense of openness, and influence the size and form of the object. They also found that red colours had a more activating effect on subjects.

2.3 Real Rooms with Complex Interactions

Billger has studied colour in real rooms in terms of the complex interactions between form, light and colour [18, 19]. Her interest has been in colour appearance, colour change and colour description using complete rooms and artificial light. Billger emphasised the direct attention and conscious reflection of subjects when in rooms, finding it valuable to use subject's verbal descriptions on colour appearance.

Hårleman accomplished two full-scale studies on colour appearance in natural daylight. Both studies concerned north and south-facing rooms, and involved yellowish/bluish [20-22] and reddish/greenish [23] colours in two nuances. Stahre *et al.* [24] compared two previous studies on associations and emotional response on colours: Hårleman's 2004 room study [23] and a study using colour patches [14]. It showed that the colour patches had to be much more colourful to give comparable associations.

2.4 Terminology

We used the NCS system and adopted its terminology [25]. *Colour* is thus defined as: colour percept, colour observation, colour perception; that which people see as colour and make it possible to make out objects and fields on the basis of colour differences. *A hue* in the NCS system is defined according to the relation to the four elementary colours: red, blue, green, yellow. Hue relation is shown through position in the colour circle. The colour triangle shows colour *nuance*, described as parts of blackness, whiteness and chromaticness. Chromaticness is the sum of a colour's chromatic qualities. *Elementary attributes* are termed whiteness, blackness, yellowness, redness, blueness and greenness. Orange has thus two chromatic elementary attributes: yellow and red.

The term *inherent colour* is used as a base point for measuring shifts in hue and nuance. Inherent colour refers to the colour a coloured object would have if observed in standardised observation conditions as denoted for NCS colour samples in agreement with their specifications, i.e. with their colour code. This entails colour samples being placed at a 45° angle, observed in a light cabinet with simulated daylight consisting of six Luma Colorette fluorescent lights at 5400 K [25,26]. Inherent colour is a constant characteristic independent of external circumstances, assuming requirements are adhered to. Inherent colour is compared to the identity colour that arises. The term *identity colour*, as developed by Billger, is a term which tallies with a holistic attitude and should thus be interpreted as the main impression of what is apprehended as a single-coloured surface in a room. The term *experience* is used as an everyday term for mental and emotional excitation. Such experience can consist of feelings or emotional states, which arise in the experimental room. These experiences or emotional states may consist of memories, associations and metaphors. *Room character* here functions as an overriding term for evaluation of a room with light, colour, space, surfaces and other architectonic elements. Finally, *colour connotation, as* Sivik and Taft defined it, is words having meaning not primarily related to colour [6]. We use colour connotations for the idea or meaning suggested by or associated with a colour, a room colour or a colour word.

3 STUDY DESIGN

3.1 Design Approach

The experimental period was June to September in Stockholm, where the sun rises between 0334 and 0634 hours and sets between 2205 and 1845. The intention with the study design was to create an environmental colour design in order to catch reactions to room and colour as subtle descriptions. The main focus during the sessions was to supply the subjects with a *standard situation*, in this case a calm and 'normal' (in contrast to experimental) situation, a pause for reflection permitting them to focus on room and colour. In total, 72 subjects made 118 observations. Sky conditions for each session were stated in a questionnaire. The methodology was designed for separate sequences, and to put subjects at ease in the experimental situation.

3.2 Subjects and Experimental Rooms

Subjects were architects and interior designers, plus students reading these subjects. This choice of professional category, with people interested in both colour and spaces, was made so as to obtain, as far as possible, informed and detailed descriptions[1]. Each observer gave two complete descriptions of colour appearance, one in each room. These together took over one hour and during that time four further part-studies were made.

Two similar full-scale rooms were set up in a construction cabin positioned facing north–south. The cabin was placed in a slope, with vegetation in front of the room in sunlight and other houses with yellow plaster outside the room in skylight. Room measurements were 4.2 × 2.9 m. The inner surface of the walls consisted of plywood roller-painted with a new inherent colour for each test sequence. Floors were covered with beige-speckled lino, and ceilings were white-painted. Both rooms had

1. The subjects were a rather homogenous group and it was not intended to use observer's age and gender statistically. It so happened that it was more females in the beginning and more students in the end why there is no use in comparing age, gender and occupation.

similar short-end windows with white-painted frames and inner reveals. The natural daylight was transmitted from clear, double-glazed panes. The colour temperature in the rooms on a fairly cloudy day was approx 8000 K in the north-facing and approx 7000 K in the south-facing room (figure 1).

3.3 Colour Selection

The colours chosen were three pinkish and three greenish hues in two nuances commonly used in architectural and interior colour designs. They were chosen to have perceptual equal distance[2]. The nuances were whitish 1010 and more chromatic 1030. The hues were yellowish-pink (Y80R), pink (R), bluish-pink (R20B), bluish-green (B70G), green (G) and yellowish-green (G20Y). Due to unsuitable weather conditions for a lengthy period, the pale yellowish-green colour (1010-G20Y) was omitted. One yellowish and one bluish inherent colour that were used in a previous study were included [20-22]. These colours, reddish-yellow (1030-Y20R) and reddish-blue (1030-R80B), showed interesting patterns of hue shift, and could serve as reference points between the studies. Used colours are shown in figures 2 and 3. CIELAB coordinates for the used colours are given in Table A.

Table A. CIELAB coordinates for the used NCS colours

NCS	L D65,10	a D65,10	b D65,10
S 1010-Y80R	84,67	6,72	7,44
S 1010-R	83,39	5,72	3,63
S 1010-R20B	84,33	6,24	0,04
S 1010-B70G	85,94	-6,66	0,28
S 1010-G	85,43	-7,37	3,73
S 1030-B70G	81,17	-20,85	-0,04
S 1030-G	79,94	-20,33	9,89

2. In the NCS colour system colours are arranged according to similarity with the elementary colours: white, black, yellow, red, blue and green. As a consequence, the NCS system does not define equal distance between elementary colours, and the colour circle has in fact less perceptual difference between colours in the blue-green quadrant than in the others. Consequently, we have chosen to adjust that situation by selecting one green inherent colour at a larger distance from the elementary green, 30 steps instead of 20.

S 1030-G20Y	80,03	-17,57	17,65
S 1030-Y20R	82,50	9,29	34,42
S 1030-Y80R	74,83	21,74	16,21
S 1030-R	75,47	21,31	7,12
S 1030-R20B	75,80	18,92	-0,05
S 1030-R80B	77,25	-3,57	-17,91

3.4 Empirical Methods

Room and colour were observed and evaluated with qualitative methods, such as *semantic scales* and *verbal description.* We have used four out of five factors developed by Hogg *et al.*: *temperature, emotional tone, spatial quality,* and *dynamic factor* [8][3]. Established items for spatial experience were selected and grouped hypothetically under these factors. Two new variables for experience were added to the already established, *embracing* and *elevating*, associated with the emotional factor. The semantic scales were graded from zero to six, with six being the maximum, covering a value from 'not at all' to a value 'to a high degree', i.e. a type called *Likert scales* and not semantic differentials in the sense that they covered a scale from one position to its opposite. The use of Likert - scales allows a better control and thus higher data quality. Table B show items in the original grouping.

Table B. Selected items grouped in original factors

Temperature	Emotional	Spatial	Dynamic
Warm	Merry	Distinct	Elevating
Cold	Sombre	Open	Vivid
Sunny	Hard	Embracing	Tranquil
	Pleasant	Small	
	Formal		
	Dry		

3. The fourth factor, *complexity,* was not selected as it did not seem adequate in the unfurnished building shed.

A parallel method for verbal description was developed to catch the initial experience of room and colour. Subjects were encouraged to note down own thoughts and descriptive words. The given tasks were two-fold:

1. Describe your impression of the wall colour
2. Describe your impression of the room character.

The room description was the preferred option and the wall colour description was used as a complement. The subjects were instructed verbally to take their time for the process of experience and association. It was important that first impressions should not be by-passed and that evaluations and experience of the room were allowed to develop. Just as eyes must adapt to a light situation, so must experience as a whole have time to adapt in a certain spatial situation.

3.5 Procedure

The walls in two full-scale rooms were painted in the same inherent colour. Most sessions were separate but occasionally two subjects were present. After completion, the subject moved to the second room and the process was repeated. The subjects stayed in each room without any interruption, in order to adapt to prevailing light and experiment situation. Observation was thus confined to one room at a time. The adaptation to room light conditions as well as the session was made seated on a bench in a definite position with a good overview of the room. The experiment supervisor guided the subjects through the process and subsequent questionnaire, and instructed the subject to reflect on the impression that room had made. In the initial phase verbal description was performed, following by a period when more concentrated attention was required. Subjects noted their experience with a value for each item and 16 different items were used.

3.6 Methods of Analysis

Data was accumulated from studies in rooms illuminated from two different compass directions, and with six colour hues in two nuances. Data were processed statistically using the SPSS statistical program.

To reduce data, factor analysis was applied on the whole data set, using data from all inherent colours. This method generated new variables for further analyses.

Differences in evaluation between rooms in different colours and orientations were analysed by *t*-tests. In order to test the effect on evaluation by colour and orientation respectively an analysis of variance was carried out. To accentuate differences in factor loadings a Varimax Rotation was applied.

Verbal descriptions from the studies were made use of. The most frequently used expressions (at least five appearances) where put into three groups, one for each of the compass directions north and south respectively, and one group for expressions in common to both.

4 STUDY RESULTS

4.1 New Variables for Room Character[4]

The factor analysis was carried out for all observations, through all hues and nuances, using the principal components extraction method. Using Varimax Rotation, five new components with eigenvalues greater than 1 where constructed. The first three explained in all 54.6% of the total variance, together with the remaining two they explained 67.7% of the total variance. The percentage under the name of the component shows the amount of variance explained by the component respectively. In Table C the grouping of new variables is presented.

Table C. Factor matrix of room character. Rotated Component Matrix

Items	Component 1	Comp. 2	Comp. 3	Comp. 4	Comp. 5
Explained variance	31,3 %	13,6 %	9,7 %	6,7 %	6,4 %
	1	2	3	4	5
Elevating	,805	-,274	-,086	,134	,191
Merry	,796	-,302	,113	-,054	,098
Vivid	,728	-,176	,041	-,342	,367
Sunny	,687	-,083	,043	,163	-,167
Pleasant	,600	-,333	-,231	,500	,074

4. New variables are reduced calculations of items.

Warm	,456	(-,623)	,174	,128	-,148
Sombre	(-,693)	,164	,146	,212	-,093
Hard	-,170	,782	-,052	-,251	,041
Cold	-,286	,741	-,114	,041	,090
Formal	-,196	,607	-,189	,143	-,201
Dry	-,005	,569	,422	,368	-,118
Embracing	-,095	-,294	,703	,077	,321
Small	,215	-,022	,597	-,230	-,153
Open	,389	,115	(-,664)	,316	,033
Tranquil	-,055	-,016	-,198	,821	-,006
Distinct	,165	,045	,004	,007	,881

(Extraction Method: Principal Component Analysis. Rotation Method: Varimax with Kaiser Normalization.)

Following the factor analysis, four new variables were constructed to reduce data. The values of these four new variables were calculated as the mean of the included items [27]. Items with negative factor loadings were not included in the calculation: working as mirror images of their opposites they would have confounded the values of factor variables by levelling out the calculated mean values. Included variables have factor loadings over 0,40. Greatest factor loadings are arranged on top. New variables and characterization based on included items are presented in Table D.

Table D. New variables for room character

Elevating	Harsh	Embracing	Peaceful
Elevating	Hard	Embracing	Tranquil
Merry	Cold	Small	Pleasant
Vivid	Formal	Dry	
Sunny	Dry		
Pleasant			
Warm			

The first two variables describe two different attitudes towards the room, a positive and a negative. Temperature goes together with other emotional expressions: warm, sunny, merry, elevating respectively cold, harsh, formal and dry. The third variable describes an embracing spatial experience, maybe even tight or narrow. The fourth variable brings about a positive sense of peace, a mood, where pleasant is included as in the first variable. The fifth variable represents only distinct and has low correlation with the other variables, which makes *distinct* a specific attribute on its own.

4.2 Impact Caused by Colour or Orientation

The impact of hue and orientation on spatial experience was assessed by *t*-tests. Table E shows comparisons between categories and sub-categories made up by orientation and colour. The comments on *more* or *less* show the directions of the differences. Test (A) concerns orientation only: all cases are compared divided in north- and south room categories. Test (B) concerns colour and orientation: all cases divided in pink and green categories are compared to the orientation categories. Test (C) concerns colour and orientation: all cases divided in smaller colour categories are compared to the orientation categories. Test (D) concerns only pinkish colours and orientation: a yellowish pink and a bluish pink category are compared to the orientation categories.

There were some significant differences in the perception of the rooms, but mostly the difference between different inherent colours overpowered the difference between the identity colours from the same inherent colour (test B1 and C1). Using the whole data set there was an indication, but not statistically significant (Z), that the orientation facing north was less related to an elevating character. When the data set was grouped into sub-samples of colour in two nuances, this difference was significant for the group consisting of yellowish-pinks and bluish-greens[5].

Pink rooms were evaluated as less 'harsh' and more 'embracing' than were green rooms. The 'embracing' character includes an allusion to a cramped condition, and this was more explicit in both pink and yellowish pink rooms than in green and bluish-green rooms. Also the pink rooms were perceived as more distinct than

5. Using the whole dataset the inherent colours were contra productive and the smaller groups tended to be too small for statistics.

the green ones. Comparison between the sub-group yellowish-pink and bluish-pink did not show any significant difference.

4.3 Effects Due to Hue and Orientation

A two-way analysis of variance was used to explain the effects of colour in relation to the effects of orientation, and their mutual interaction. The variables studied were the same as in the *t*-tests: elevating, harsh, embracing, peaceful and distinct. In Table F.1 numbers in boldface manifest significant connections, numbers in italics are nearly significant. Table F.2 presents the proportions of variance explained.

The analysis showed an explicit effect by differences in colour. Regarding pink and green hues, the main part of the variance explained stemmed from different hues. It means that differences between room evaluations are greater between red and green colours than between different orientations. Generally, the nuance 1030 did affect both positive and negative emotional items more than the lighter 1010 nuances.

4.4 Colour Connotations in Verbal Description

The subjects used a variety of expressions to describe room character and differences between them. Most obvious was that greenish and pinkish rooms evoked different colour connotations. Pinkish rooms caused associations of human skin, facial colour, strong emotional expressions such as affection and defiance and other mental characteristics, while greenish rooms caused associations of nature that could be either pure nature or artificial. Within these fields of associations subjects had all sorts of different perspectives.

Some subjects described the pinkish rooms as warm, gentle and stimulating but others experienced those rooms as pushy, demanding and glaring. Some experienced them as childish, young, fresh and funny while yet others described them as stale, tasteless, vulgar and slovenly. Pinkish rooms produced various images of skin (dressed or naked, of small children or adults), and views varied on whether they were sweet or trying, innocent or sinful.

Greenish colour connotations were of a completely different kind. Greenish rooms evoked connotations of nature, and relaxation. These rooms projected a shadow, an image of a landscape, or an unrestricted space. This in turn caused

spatial quality. They are not comparable with the original factors as they emerge from different ways of analysing data. The 'elevating' variable was essential in describing room character; warm colours and the more chromatic nuances increase happy and pleasing emotional experiences. The 'distinct' variable correlated well with the observation of warm colours as proceeding while the cold ones seem to be receding. As the cold bluish and greenish walls seemed to withdraw they consequently made an indistinct impression.

5.3 Comparisons between Studies

Pink aroused strongest emotional reactions, regarding both positive and negative character. The conclusion of Hogg *et al.* that the warmth factor more often expresses an emotional tone than strict temperature is confirmed [8]. Sivik has also pointed out that pink, and in particular bluish-pink, is often described in negative terms such as ugly, disagreeable and unappetising [5]. We can see a clear relationship between these negative evaluations from pink colour samples and room character.

The new variable 'embracing', previously belonging to the emotional factor, was grouped together with the terms small and closed (not open). This tallies well with Küller's conclusion concerning the word-scales closed/airy and small/large, as being not fully correlated [11]. Rooms assessed as large could just as well be perceived as enclosed. Evidently 'embracing' is not only a spatial scale for emotional tone but also for a cramped sense.

However, trying to find connections between items and factors can be hazardous. Since many items often compose a factor, it is hard to find a perfect name that entirely encapsulates the true content. There is no standard procedure to help with the naming process and this makes it even more difficult to compare connections between colour emotion factors and colour attributes. A clearly positive evaluation in preference for warm colours did crystallise. This could be expected with subjects as a cross-section of the population but is an interesting result for architects and student architects. This unexpected tendency is worth noting as several researchers have presented evidence that the colour preferences of architects often differ from those of non-architects, the former often preferring stricter and cooler objects [8,28]. This might indicate a wider application of the results presented.

6 CONCLUSION

The methods used in this study have helped to explore people's experience of room and colour, resulting in three new variables that can be applied to the experience of room character: elevating, harsh and embracing.

The study present offers a new perspective for colour experience in rooms. We were able to undertake a great amount of systematic evaluation that could be arranged into a bigger pattern, thus making it easier to grasp connections between visual appearance and evaluation of colour.

Hue and nuance clearly rendered a common experience in colour connotations. Spatial evaluation was firmly bound to the identity colour. Pinkish and greenish colours caused almost opposing room characters. The difference between warm and cold colours was clearest.

Light from different compass directions resulted in variances in room character. As north- and south-facing rooms of the same inherent colour gain different identity colours, such rooms make different impacts and subjects react differently. The direction of illumination affected spatial character, by means of a strengthening or weakening of colour attribute. To some degree, the north-facing and south-facing aspects imposed their own spatial characters.

7 REFERENCES

[1] C E Osgood, P H Tannenbaum and G J Suci, *The measurement of meaning* (Urbana: University of Illinois Press, 1957).

[2] B Wright and L Rainwater, *J. General Psychol.*, **67** (1962) 89-99.

[3] J A Hogg, *J. General Psychol.*, **80** (1969) 129-140.

[4] S Kobayashi, *Col. Res. Appl.,* **6**, (2) (1981) 93-107.

[5] L Sivik, Proc. AIC Color 69, Stockholm, **1/2** (1969) 1064-1072.

[6] L Sivik and C Taft, *Colour combinations and associated meanings – semantic dimensions and colour chords,* Psychological Reports, Volume 1 (Gothenburg: University of Gothenburg, 1992).

[7] R Küller, Doctoral dissertation, National Swedish Institute for Building Research, Stockholm (1972).

[8] J Hogg, S Goodman, T Porter, B Mikkelides and D E Preddy, *Br. J. Psychol.*, **70**

(1979) 231-242.

[9] M Kunishima and T Yanase, *Ergonomics*, **28** (6) (1985) 869-882.

[10] R Küller in *Architecture for people*, Ed. B Mikkelides (New York: Holt, Rinehart and Winston, 1980). ISBN 0-03-057491-9

[11] R Küller, *J. Light Vis. Environment*, **10** (2) (1986) 33-37.

[12] R Küller in *Environment, cognition and action*, Ed. T Gärling and G Evans (New York: Oxford University Press, 1991). ISBN 0-19-506220-5

[13] B Mikellides, Doctoral dissertation, Oxford Polytechnic (1989).

[14] T Sato, K Kajiwara, H Hoshino and T Nakamura, *Adv. Col. Sci. Technol.*, **3** (2000) 53–59.

[15] L Oberasher and M Gallmetzer, Proc. AIC 2003, Bangkok (2003).

[16] L C Ou, M R Luo, A Woodcock, and A Wright, *Col. Res. Appl.*, **29** (3) (2003) 232-240.

[17] L C Ou, M R Luo, A Woodcock, and A Wright, *Col. Res. Appl.*, **29** (4) (2003) 292-298.

[18] M Billger, Doctoral dissertation, Chalmers University of Technology, Gothenburg (1999). ISBN 91-7197-820 8

[19] M Billger, Proc. AIC 2004, Porto Alegre, Brazil (2004).

[20] M Hårleman, *Färg i norr- och södervettande rum: kulörtonförskjutning genom varierande ljusförhållanden* (Stockholm: Royal institute of Technology (KTH), School of Architecture, 2000); ISBN 91-7170-590-2. In Swedish.

[21] M Hårleman, *Nordic Journal of Architectural Research*, 2 (2001) 41-48.

[22] M Hårleman, Proc. AIC Color 2001, Rochester, USA, Vol. 4421 (2001) 69-71. ISBN 0-8194-4128-7

[23] M Hårleman, Proc. AIC 2004, Porto Alegre, Brazil (2004).

[24] B Stahre, M Hårleman and M Billger, Proc. AIC 2004, Porto Alegre,(2004).

[25] A Hård and L Sivik, *Col. Res. Appl.*, **6** (3) (1981).

[26] A Hård, L Sivik and G Tonnquist, *Col. Res. Appl.*, **21** (3) (1996) 180-205, 206-220.

[27] P Kline, *The handbook of psychological testing* (London: Routledge, 1995).

[28] J Janssens, *Looking at buildings – individual variations in the perception of building exteriors*, (Lund, Sweden: Lund Institute of Technology, 1984).

This is a colour of a moon shadow and into the room.

More chromatic reddish blue (S 1030-R80B) in the north

shadows,
runs around the window

ABSTRACT

A study on the emotional impact of selected colours was made. Ninety observers in 118 studies used 13 colours in two nuances. Two full- scale rooms in daylight were used with windows facing south respectively north. Dissimilar shares of sky light and sunlight causes differences in colour appearance and the question was whether these changes effect colour emotion. Furthermore, two contrary colouring methods were compared. In one method colours reinforce the light situation, in the other they neutralize it. The purpose was to investigate if these methods caused different experiences and whether one held greater appreciation. Questions are answered by analysing connections between inherent colours, compass orientations and emotional impact. The investigation showed that various colours and nuances were determinate for the emotional category. Rooms with warm colours were more appreciated than rooms with cool colours. The more chromatic nuance (NCS 1030) caused stronger emotions and different emotional chategories than the light nuance (1010). Yellow and pinkish rooms caused stronger emotional effect than greenish and a bluish colours, with regard to both positive and negative emotions. The colouring methods were differently evaluated. The reinforcing method made rooms with warm colours more appreciated. Warm colors where mostly experienced with joy, while cool colours were experienced with more acceptances. The neutralizing method caused higher values for rooms with cool colours in relation to warm colours. This method made south facing rooms in cool colours almost as appreciated as warm colours in north facing. Cool colours in both nuances held more accepting and less surprise than warm colours.

Colour Emotion in Full-Scale Rooms

Hårleman, M.

Published in AIC (Association International de la Couleur) proceedings 2004, 223-226.

1. INTRODUCTION

I present a study on emotional experiences in rooms with differing colours and compass orientations: north and south. North facing rooms are lit mostly by sky light while south facing rooms are lit mostly by sunlight. Sky light is often described as cool or neutral while sunlight is experienced as warm. This causes differences in how colours appear in the rooms and between the two rooms. In colour design, colours sometimes are used to treat scarcities in the environment or to emphasise merits. In the Nordic countries achievement of an experience of warmth might be wished for. One may want to make a cool- looking room feel warm with "warm colours,"[1] but also to cool a warm-looking room with "cool colours." The method is to use a colour to modify room light; either to reinforce the light situation or to neutralize it. Others claim that room colours will be beautiful when corresponding with colour of light; blue and green colours in a north facing room will be brilliant. The aim is to gain knowledge on how these colouring methods work. The questions are:

1. Can the colour and light situation in a room cause differences in emotional experience?
2. Does the method for reinforcing or neutralizing the light situation cause greater estimated experiences than the other? Do one or another of these methods cause dissimilar experiences?

Questions are answered by showing and analysing connections between the inherent colours, compass orientations and emotional impacts. The colouring methods

1. In a recent study (2004) I found that the yellowish and reddish colours consistently were experienced as warm, and bluish and greenish colours as cool, bluish red and yellowish green were exceptions. Differences between these groups were consistent through many dimensions, hence use of the categories warm and cool colours.

are evaluated in relation to their emotional impact. I will discuss my results in relation to Oberacher and Gallmetzer (2003). Indeed, they had colours with much stronger chromaticness but it might be interesting to compare results. Oberacher and Gallmetzer made an investigation on colour emotion using basic emotions[2] and various colour compositions. They found emotional associations from colours; yellow and red caused pleasure. Describing emotional quality, they found that small differences in association of concepts, or patterns of intermediate colours, can lead to dissimilar subjective representations. Red was associated to anger, pleasure and fear; yellow with pleasure and joy; green and pink with disgust.

2. STUDY DESIGN

The study is entitled the Red-Green Investigation, since these elementary attributes are those primarily dealt with. In the text, however, I talk about the reddish colours in terms of 'pink', since red colour in the nuances used generally is called pink. I have used the NCS system and adopt its terminology.[3] The term inherent colour is used to denote that colour which an object would have if observed under standardised observation conditions applicable when an NCS colour sample colour corresponds with its notation.[4] Identity colour is a term which should be interpreted as the main impression of what is apprehended as a single-coloured surface in a room.[5] Ninety observers made 118 studies. Two similar full-scale rooms were set up in a construction cabin positioned facing north- south. Room measurements were 4.20 m x 2.90 m with similar short-end windows. The walls were roller-painted and three reddish and three greenish hues in two nuances were chosen in nuances commonly used in interiors. Nuances were 1010 and 1030. The hues were yellow-red (Y80R), red (R), blue-red (R20B), blue-green (B70G), green (G) and yellow-green (G20Y). The inherent colours red-yellow (1030-Y20R) and red-blue (1030-R80B) were also used. The observers made two complete studies in each room. These together took over one

2. The basic emotions (Ekman) are quite similar to the primary emotions (Plutchik) I use. Basic emotions do not include anticipation, but instead contempt.
3. Hård and Sivik (1981)
4. Fridell Anter (2000).
5. Billger (1999).

hour. The identity colour of the walls was compared with colour samples placed in a colour reference box[6]. The NCS notation was recorded in a questionnaire by the test supervisor. To classify emotions I used a method by the American psychologist and researcher Robert Plutchik (1962, 1980). Plutchik found eight primary emotions: fear, anger, sadness, joy, acceptance, disgust, anticipation and surprise.[7] A semantic differential scale was used. For methodological reasons I have split the (primary) emotions into positive and negative categories. The positive category consists of joy, acceptance, anticipation and surprise, and in the negative one I placed fear, anger, sadness and disgust. Data was processed in simple frequency analyses and presented as mean values.

3. RESULTS

Acceptance, surprise, joy and anticipation made up the majority of reactions in the rooms. Rooms with warm colours were generally higher evaluated than rooms with cool colours. The more chromatic nuance (1030) made stronger impression and where more appreciated than the light nuance (1010). Warm, pinkish colours in 1030 nuance caused most joy and cool colours caused most acceptances. Reddish blue and bluish green caused most acceptances of all colours. Pinkish colours also caused much surprise and anticipation. The reddish yellow colour (1030-Y20R) caused the strongest positive reactions of all colours. Light greenish colours, on the other hand, caused less surprise than the more chromatic greenish colours and only weak negative emotions. North facing rooms in yellowish colours; yellowish green and yellowish red (1030-G20Y and 1030-Y80R and 1010-Y80R) was less appreciated, while the same room in the more chromatic reddish yellow (1030-Y20R) was more appreciated. Almost all rooms evoked some negative emotion, mostly disgust. Rooms with warm colours in the more chromatic nuance (1030-Y80R, -R and -G20Y) evoked disgust and anger, while the more chromatic cool colours (1030-R20B, -R80B, B70G and -G) caused disgust and sadness. Pink with elmentary red

6. Billger and Hårleman (1999)
7. Primary emotions are emotional manifestations as most adults, disregarding culture and education are familiar with. The method has been previously used be the swedish researcher and architect Sven Hesselgren in studies on emotions in built environment. Hesselgren used a five graded scale while I used a ten graded scale.

hue (1030-R) caused the most negative emotions. Rooms with bluish pink caused less negative emotions than with the other pinks. Rooms with pinkish colours in the light nuance (1010) caused more acceptances and less joy than with the 1030 nuance. The former colours also evoked more sadness and less disgust.

The colouring method using inherent colours in reinforcing room- light, made the highest appreciated studies. Warm colours were higher evaluated than cool colours and higher with the reinforcing method than with the neutralizing. The neutralizing method made south facing rooms in cool colours almost as appreciated as warm colours in north facing. Warm colors where mostly experienced with joy, while cool colours where experienced with more acceptances. Warm colours also evoked more anticipation and surprise. Cool colours in both nuances held more accepting and less surprise than warm colours.

4. DISCUSSION

Yellow and pink caused pleasure and evenmore joy. Describing emotional quality, I found, like Oberascher and Gallmetzer, that small colour shifts can lead to shifts also in the emotional chategories. Pink was associated to anger and pleasure as red was in the Oberasher and Gallmetzer study and yellow was associated with pleasure and joy. In that respect, my pink rooms correspond better with their results on red (anger; pleasure; fear) and purple (sadness, lonelyness, depression). Likewise green and pink was associated with disgust, thou pink in my study, had the highest value in disgust as in joy, anticipation and surprise. This richness in variety differs from Oberascher and Gallmetzer´s study, where pink merely associated to disgust. Similarly, green is not in accordance with my result. In the Oberasher and Gallmetzer study, green evoked emotions of disgust, while in my study it caused merely acceptance.

I found it interesting with the strong and differing opinions on pink. The subjects where divided in two groups, but in all cases, both groups used positive and negative primary emotions. The group with a more negative attitude towards the pink room often felt surprise or anticipation together with disgust, fear and sadness. The positive group often felt joy and surprise together with disgust or sadness. Finally, I want to discuss the primary emotions in relation to the room study. The problem is what these (primary) emotions express in such a study. I try to interpret contribution and relevance according to this study. Evaluations for surprise and anticipation were high, together with joy and acceptance. Surprise may reflect a beautiful or astonishing impression. Anticipation may imply a curiosity towards colour and room – thoughts on how this impression can remain under the influence of daily life, and may thereby reflect a cautious prediction regarding this, or just a wish to use the same colour. The negative category is represented by strong expressions, a bit too strong to be used for anything so ordinary and harmless as the wall colour in a small and simple, almost unfurnished room. This is particularly the case with fear, but also with disgust, anger and sadness. Some observers commented on this. But still these rooms were able to evoke emotions and associations of the same kind.

5. CONCLUSIONS

The reinforcing light situations, were highest evaluated concerning warm colours, while the neutralizing light situations, caused as high values for cool colours as warm colours. The conclusion is that though warmth is preferred, the room situation can be influenced with colours. Yet, it can be seen, that altough the temperature factor is important, the bluish rooms still where much appreciated.

Pale and greenish colours caused weaker emotional impact than more chromatic, bluish, yellowish and pinkish colours. This was also a question of different emotional categories; from joy to acceptance, from anger and disgust to sadness.

6. REFERENCES

Billger, M., and Hårleman, M., 1999. "A method for comparison of colour appearance in differently illuminated rooms". In CIE 24th session proceedings. Publ. no. 133, Vol.1- part 1.

Hesselgren, S. 1987. *On architecture : an architectural theory based on psychological research.* Bromley: Chartwell- Bratt. ISBN 0-86238-094-4

Hård, A., and Sivi, L., 1981. NCS- Natural Colour System: A Swedish standard for colour notation. Color Research and Application 6 (3): 129- 138.

Hårleman, M. 2004. "Significance of Colour on Spatial Character", unpublished dissertation manuscript, planned publication in short at Royal Institute of Technology, Stockholm.[8]

Oberasher, L., and Gallmetzer, M. 2003, "Colour and Emotion". In Proceedings AIC Color 2003. ed. by A. Hansuebsai. Bangkok: Chulalongkorn university, p. 370-375.

Plutchik, R.,1962. *The Emotions: Facts, Theories, and a New Model*. New York: Studies in psychology.

Plutchik, R., 1994. *The Psychology and Biology of Emotion*. New York: Harper Collins College Publishers.

7. ACKNOWLEDGMENTS

This work has been supported with a grant from The Swedish Research Council for Environment, Agricultural Sciences and Spatial Planning and the Swedish Association of Painting Contractors.

8. Paper 4 in this publication.

**A warm light blue,
Silent, clean, smooth.
A mild and pleasurable
In here rests a nursing,
without worry and severity.**

Light greenish blue (S 1010-B30G) in the North.

a Madonna blue.
Embracing, even enveloping.
colour to hold by the hand.
almost pious atmosphere,

ABSTRACT

It is well known that a colour's appearance can differ between a small colour chip and the same colour applied to a real room. The impression of the colour changes between these circumstances; e.g. on the chip it can be subdued, while it is perceived as striking in the room. In this paper, we compare the results of a colour chip study, Colour Emotion, to Hårleman's full-scale room study.

In the first study, textile chips were viewed against a grey background in a viewing cabinet. In the other study, two rooms were painted in 12 hues in two different nuances: NCS 1010 and NCS 1030. They correspond well to the hue areas and to two of the nuance categories used in the chip study. Semantic scaling was used in both studies. The two studies show a distinct difference between words associated to colours of the same nuance and colour category. A clear pattern could be seen. In the room, the colours were perceived as more distinct, stronger and they arouse much stronger emotions. Generally, a colour chip had to be much more colourful to give comparable associations.

Colour Emotions in Larger and Smaller Scale

Stahre, B, Hårleman, M and Billger, M.

Published in AIC proceedings 2004, pp. 27-30.

1. INTRODUCTION

How does the context affect our associations towards colour? It is a well-known fact that the colour experience differs, depending on whether it is applied to a small surface or to a whole room. In this text, two studies will be compared. One is Maud Hårleman's investigation into the colour experience in painted rooms, lit by daylight in north- and southfacing direction (Hårleman 2001, 2004). The other study is the Swedish part of the international project colour Emotion Research and Application (Billger, Stahre and Konradsson 2002).

The aim is to describe differences and similarities in the way we percieve colours, on the basis of the context's significance and the size of the colour field. In this text, only the results from the north facing room in Hårlemans study will be compared with the colour samples of the Colour emotion study, due to the fact that this is the light best resembling neutral light.

2. METHODS

2.1. Hårleman's room-study

In her investigations, Hårleman has conducted studies in two full-scale rooms with similar colour schemes, observed in light from the north and south. Her question is whether the rooms get a different character through the differences in colour the light creates. Additionally six hues in two nuances were used for painting the rooms; 3 light pink, 3 pink, 2 light green and 3 green paints, and a yellow and a blue. 90

observers carried out a total of 118 studies.[1]

Semantic differential scales, graded from one to six, have been used to describe the character of the rooms, complemented with oral interviews. The meaning of the different significant variables on the differential scales have over the years been tested by many researchers (Kunishima & Yanase 1985, Küller 1980, 1991, Sivik & Taft 1992). It has been determined that they sort under different factors for different research fields, like colour in room-model, exterior-colour, single colours and colour combinations. Hogg et al. (1979) discovered five factors which concern colour in room-models. In Hårleman's room study, four of these have been used to sort the different variables of experience. These factors are: *temperature* (cold, warm); *spacial quality* (small, clear, open, dry, hard); *dynamism* (tranquil, lively) and *emotional tone* (gloomy, cheerful, nice, formal, sunny). In addition, two untested variables of experience have been added (surrounding and elevating). These sort under the factor *emotional tone*.[2]

2.2. The Colour Emotion-Study

During the spring of 2002, the Swedish part of the international Colour emotion-study was carried out at Chalmers, which aimed to investigate how people from different contries and cultures associate towards colours. The study was led by Tetsuya Sato of the Kyoto Institute of Technology and Jim Nobbs of the University of Leeds. In all of the countries 114 colour chips, in 10-12 nuances of 10 hues, were used along with 6 acromatic samples. The colour samples were observed against a neutral grey background in a viewing cabinet with simulated (D65). In the Swedish part of the study 60 observers participated, with equal numbers of men and women.

A semantic 2-point method was used for the assessment, which meant that the observers chose which word in a word-pair corresponded most with the colour. The translation of the Japanese words was done in each country. In Sweden a translation was done based upon both Japanese and English. Twelve word-pairs were used in the study: Deep-Pale, Dynamic-Passive, Distinct-Vague, Gaudy-Plain,

1. Correct number is 72 observers.
2. Surrounding factor was later named embracing factor.

Heavy-Light, Light-Dark, Soft-Hard, Striking-Subdued, Strong-Weak, Transparent-Turbid, Vivid-Dull and Warm-Cold.

2.3. Comparison of the Two Studies

How can the different studies be compared? The Colour emotion-study (CE) has more adjectives describing each colour, while the room study focuses more on the feelings and experiences of the room. Often we cannot compare the studies word for word, however we can translate the words to reasonably correlate with the other study and thus gain a picture of how the colours were percieved in the different situations. Also if we gather the descriptive adjectives from each study, we get a collection of impressions which together provide us with a clearer picture for comparison.

The two studies are based upon two different colour order systems. In the room-study the NCS-system was used and the CE-study used the system SCOTDIC PLUS 2000, which is based on Munsell's colour order system and adjusted to textile samples. To make the comparison between the two studies correct, we have visually translated the textile chips into the NCS-system (see figure 1).

3. RESULTS

In Hårleman's room-study it was the the *pink* and *green* colours that caused the strongest experiences. These experiences were distinctly different and associated to different aspects. The green rooms were experienced as open, tranquil and lacking cheerfulness, as well as more formal and hard. The light green rooms were experienced to be cooler and more open, while the green rooms were relatively warmer and more surrounding. The blue-green room however, was experienced to be the coldest. The pink rooms were perceived to be neither formal nor tranquil and gave a cheerful impression. They gave a surrounding and lively feel and were also the colours which the observers reacted strongest to in the study. All of the pink rooms were described as warm, except for the bluish pink, which was described as cold. The light pink and the pink rooms offered a similar experience, while the light green and the green rooms differed.

The differences between the pink colours in the room-study and the samples closest to them in the CE-study is striking. The light pink CE-samples are more colourful than the colours in the room-study, but were experienced as weak, subdued, fairly passive and calm. Half of the observers also described it as a cold colour. The pink hues correspond in the CE-study to three colour chips, of which one is somewhat greyer and the two others a lot more colourful. What is interesting is that the more colourful samples correspond a lot better to the room-study. They were perceived as dynamic, striking, vivid, strong, soft and gaudy. The same *inherent colour*[3] on a small textile sample were thus experienced as a weaker colour, which did not cause as strong reactions as the corresponding colours in the room-study. In the CE-study also more colourfulness in the samples was needed for the reddish colours to be experienced as warm. The lighter nuance 1010- was experienced as colder than the nuance 1030- in the room-study. This corresponds to that whiteish colours were in general experienced as colder than the more colourful samples in the CE-study. Of the textile samples we here refer to, only the colourful pink was experienced as warm in the CE-study.

In the room-study both the light green and the green colours were considered tranquil, with the light green rooms more formal and tranquil than the green ones. The tendency towards less tranquility with enhanced colourfulness agrees with the results of the CE-study. This effect however seems to demand a higher colourfulness in the green room than on the textile samples. Most observers thought that the textile samples equivalent to the paint in the room were striking and gaudy, and more than half thought they were vivid.

On the other hand the resemblances are significant between the light green rooms and the colur samples closest to them in the CE-study. The rooms were experienced as open, tranquil and enhancing the boring character of the test-room. This correspond to the CE-study, were the light green textile samples were described as passive, subdued, weak and calm.

In general, the pink rooms were experienced as soft while the green rooms were neither soft nor hard. In the colour emotion-study neither the pink nor the green colour chips were experienced as clearly hard or soft.

3. *Inherent colour* is defined as the colour property of the material that does not change due to viewing and lightning conditions. Here it is used for the NCS-code of the paints and the Munsell-code of the textile chips.

4. CONCLUSIONS

In the colour emotion study, its grey frame and the viewing cabinet as well as the room surround the colour chip in general. The colours appear more subdued than in the room-study. In a room you are surrounded by colour, you are inside it. The reflections of the room enhance both the colour and the colour experience. The displacement of colour in the room-study makes them stronger in colourfulness and blackness, and will hence correspond to a different CE-sample. To compare the experience of a room-colour and a colour in the CE-study, the CE-sample must be from a significantly stronger nuance.

5. REFERENCES

Billger M, Stahre B, Konradsson Y (2002): "Colour emotions in Sweden", In: Sato T. and Hansuebsai A. (eds.), Proceedings for the International Conference on Colour Emotion Research and Application, July 5-7, Chulalongkorn Univ., Thailand; pp. 1-3.

Hårleman, M: (2001) Colour Appearance in Different Compass Orientations. *Nordisk Arkitekturforskning*. No 2, 2001.

Hårleman M.: (2004) Significance of Colour on Spatial Character, Manuscript[4]

Hogg, J: Goodman, S., Porter, T., Mikkelides, B. & Preddy, D.E: (1979) Dimensions and determinants of judgements of colour samples and a simulated interior space by architects and non- architects. *British Journal of Psychology*, 70, p 231-242.

Küller, R: (1980) Architecture and emotions. In Mikkelides, B. (Ed), *Architecture for People*. Holt, Rinehart ans Winston, New York. ISBN 0-03-057491-9.

Küller, R: (1991) Environment assessment from a neuropsychological perspective, In Gärling, T & Evans, G. (Eds), *Environment, cognition and action*. Oxford University Press, Inc. New York. ISBN 0-19-506220-5.

Kunishima, M & Yanase, T: (1985) Visual effects of wall colours in living rooms. *Ergonomics* vol 28, No 6, p 869-882.

Sivik, L & Taft, C: (1992) *Colour combinations and associated meanings – semantic*

4. Paper 4 in this publication.

dimensions and colour chords. University of Göteborg. Göteborgs Psychological Reports. Volume nr.1.

Address: Beata Stahre, Design and Media, Architecture
Chalmers University of Technology, S– 412 96 Göteborg, Sweden
E-mails: bea@arch.chalmers.se, maudh@arch.kth.se, billger@arch.chalmers.se

APPENDICES

Number	Colour	Compass point	Name
Date	Time	Weather	Remaining

Main questions are:

1. Does the wall colour look different in the room in sky- light or sunlight?
2. Describe the difference.
3. Describe the room appearance (in aspects of light – and space)?

Describe your impression of the wall colour.
Use your own words

Describe the inherent colour/ which colour has been used?

Where do you look to decide this?
NCS- colour code:

Contemplate the wall colour concerning variations in these aspects:

Hue:
Chromaticness:
Blackness:
Whiteness:
Lightness:
Clarity/ greyish:
Where is the colour most chromatic?
Where is the colour least chromatic?

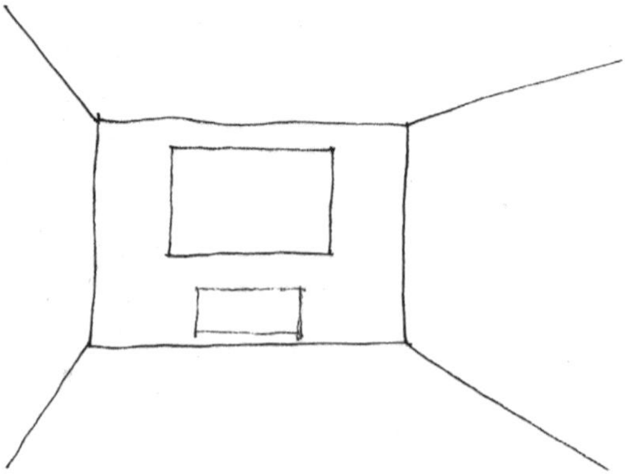

<u>Describe the colour of the wall concerning colour variations</u>
Decide a NCS- colour code of this colour using the colour reference box.

Window wall:

Long wall:

Short wall:

The colour gestalt/ character. How are the coloured walls experienced?
(Ex. Filled, radiant, grey, beautiful, gloomy, screaming, dull, indeterminable.)

<u>Atmosphere of the room</u>	Cold – warm	1 x 2
	Open – closed	1 x 2
	Light – heavy	1 x 2
	Pushy – not pushy	1 x 2
	Distinct – indistinct	1 x 2

<u>Colour in the air</u>
Does the colour stay on the wall or do you feel that it "is in the air". (Colouring objects in the room).

Name Compass Point Date Time Weather Number (Colour)

EXPERIENCE OF COLOUR IN NORTH- AND SOUTH FACING ROOMS

Answer the questions as careful as possible.

ROOM 2

1. Describe the room impression. Use you own words (essays are willingly accepted)

2. Describe the atmosphere of the room. Use your own words (preferably an essay)

3. Experiencing the room brings back in me: note points from 0 – 10.

Anger
Joy
Acceptance
Surprise
Fear
Sorrow
Sadness
Disgust
Expectation

VISUAL EVALUATION

Contemplate for a moment the colour on the walls both as a whole and with its colour variations.

4. A. Describe the wall colour in verbal concerning the hue: reddish yellow etc.

B. Nuance, its chromaticness/whiteness/blackness: whitish grey green etc.

C. Compare and describe this colour with the one in the first room.

---

5. State the room identity colour using a colour matching method with colour samples in the light booth.

6. Describe the identity colour of the separate walls using colour samples on:
The window wall
The long wall
The separating wall

---

7. Room character

Distinct	0___.___.___.___.___6
Open	0___.___.___.___.___6
Embracing	0___.___.___.___.___6
Warm	0___.___.___.___.___6
Small	0___.___.___.___.___6
Nice	0___.___.___.___.___6
Tranquil	0___.___.___.___.___6
Sombre	0___.___.___.___.___6
Sunny	0___.___.___.___.___6
Uplifting	0___.___.___.___.___6
Formal	0___.___.___.___.___6
Harsh	0___.___.___.___.___6
Dry	0___.___.___.___.___6
Cold	0___.___.___.___.___6
Cheerful	0___.___.___.___.___6
Lively	0___.___.___.___.___6

8. What do you think about this colour in different hues and nuances.
In what circumstances do you like respectively, do not like it?

9. Which colours are warm respectively cold for you?

THANK YOU FOR PARTICIPATING!

FIGURES

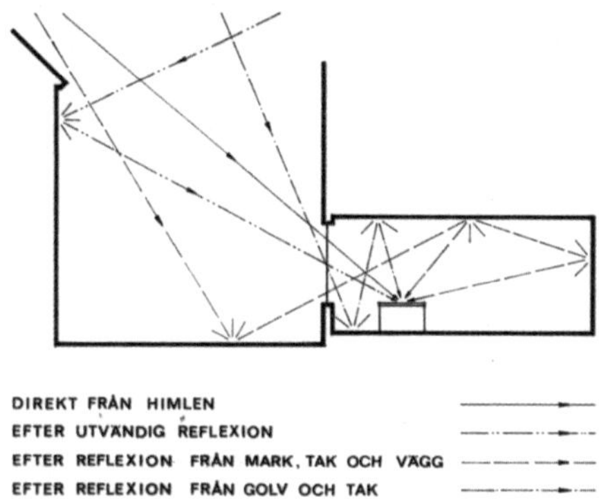

FIGURE 1. THE WAY IN WHICH DAYLIGHT REACHES A POINT IN A ROOM (FRIZELL AND LÖFBERG 1970, P. 8).

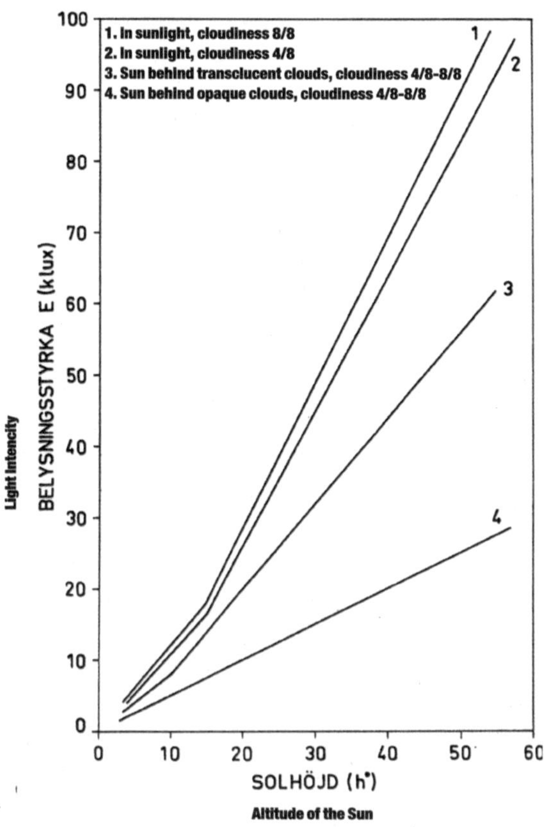

FIGURE 2. INTENSITY OF ILLUMINATION FROM SUN AND SKY IN A HORIZONTAL PLANE OUTDOORS WITH VARIED CLOUD COVER AND CLOUD TYPE (LÖFBERG 1976 P. 13).

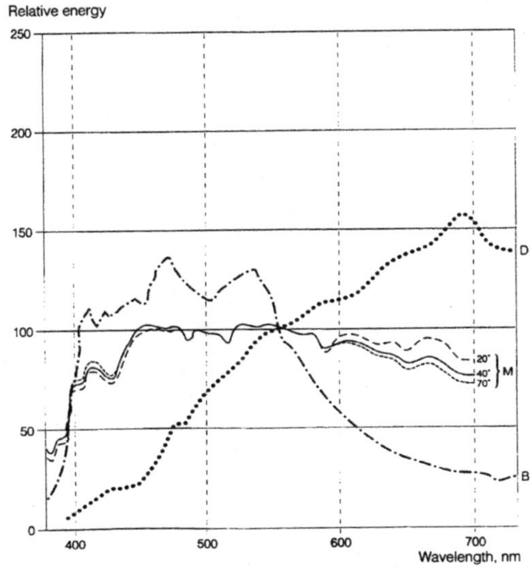

FIGURE 3. SPECTRAL COMPOSITION OF DAYLIGHT. D=DIRECT SUNLIGHT, M=OVERCAST SKY FOR DIFFERENT ALTITUDE OF THE SUN, B=BLUE SKY. (LÖFBERG 1976, P. 8, FROM FRIDELL ANTER 2000, P. 228).

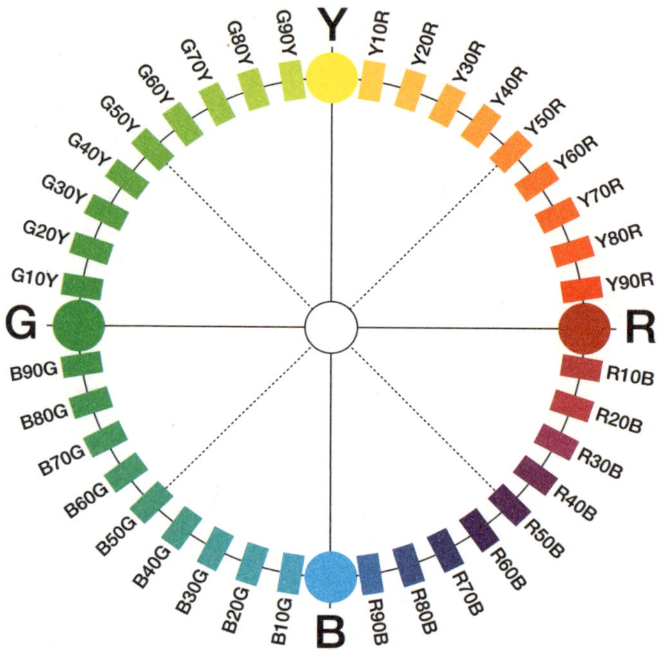

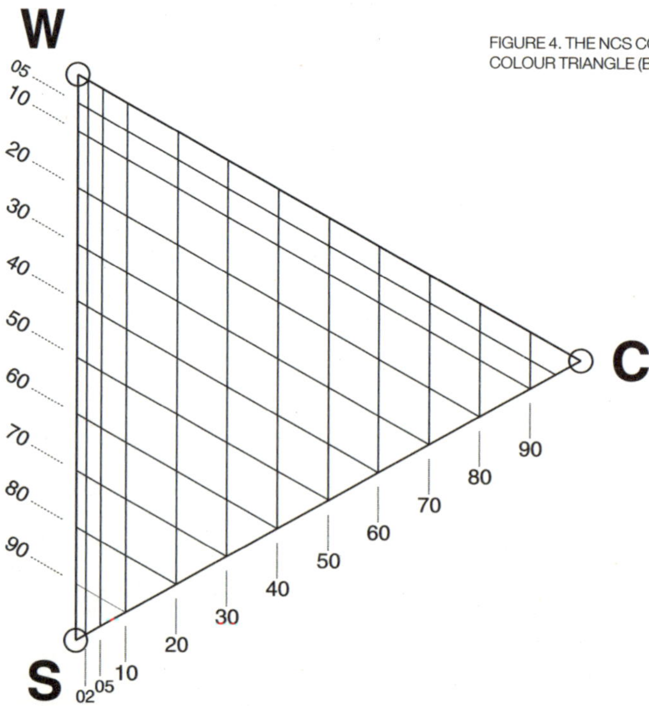

FIGURE 4. THE NCS COLOUR CIRCLE (ABOVE) AND COLOUR TRIANGLE (BELOW).

FIGURE 5. EXAMPLE OF WATERCOLOUR PAINTING USED IN PHASE ONE.
FOR EACH COLOUR REPRESENTED IN THE EXPERIMENTAL ROOMS, A WATERCOLOUR PAINTING WAS MADE AS A VISUAL MEMORY AID.

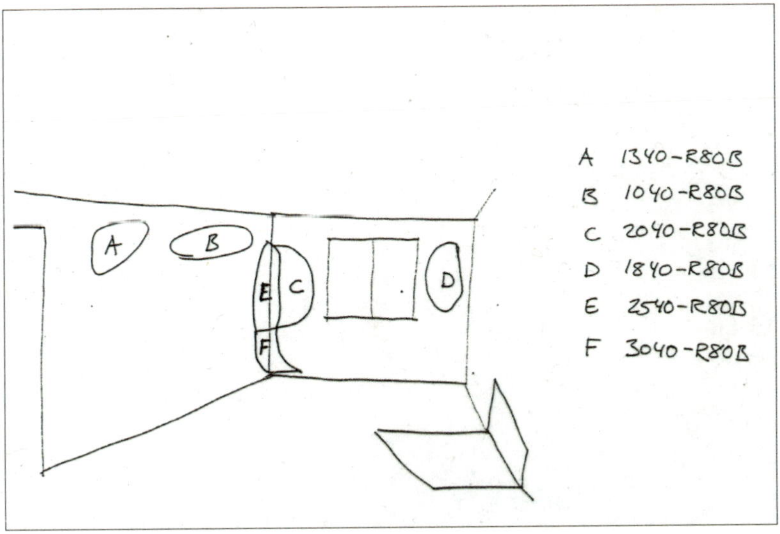

FIGURE 6. EXAMPLE OF COLOUR SCHEME USED IN PHASE ONE.
A COLOUR SCHEME WAS MADE FOR EACH STUDY INVESTIGATING THE EFFECTS SEEN IN THE VISUAL EVALUATION REGARDING AREAS OF EACH COLOUR VARIATION NOTED.

Decreased Light Intensity

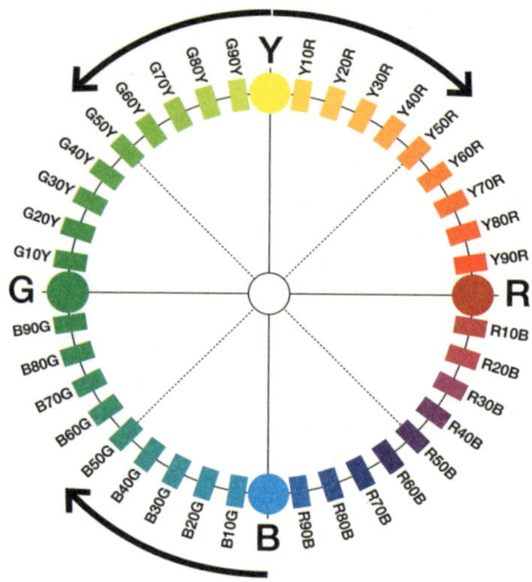

FIGURE 7. THE BEZOLD-BRÜCKE EFFECT. DECREASED LIGHT INTENSITY (TOP), INCREASED LIGHT INTENSITY (BOTTOM).

Increased Light Intensity

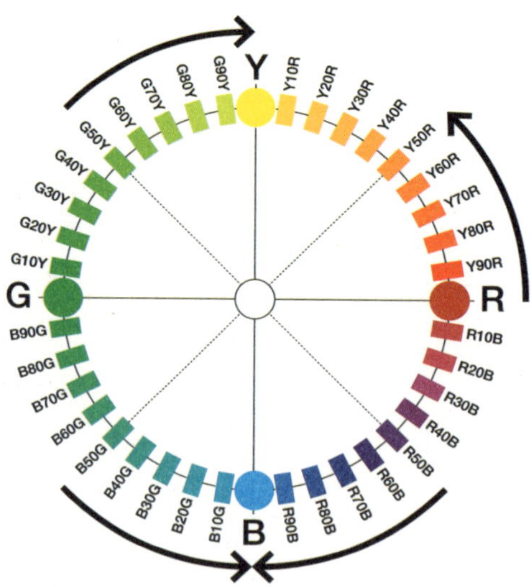

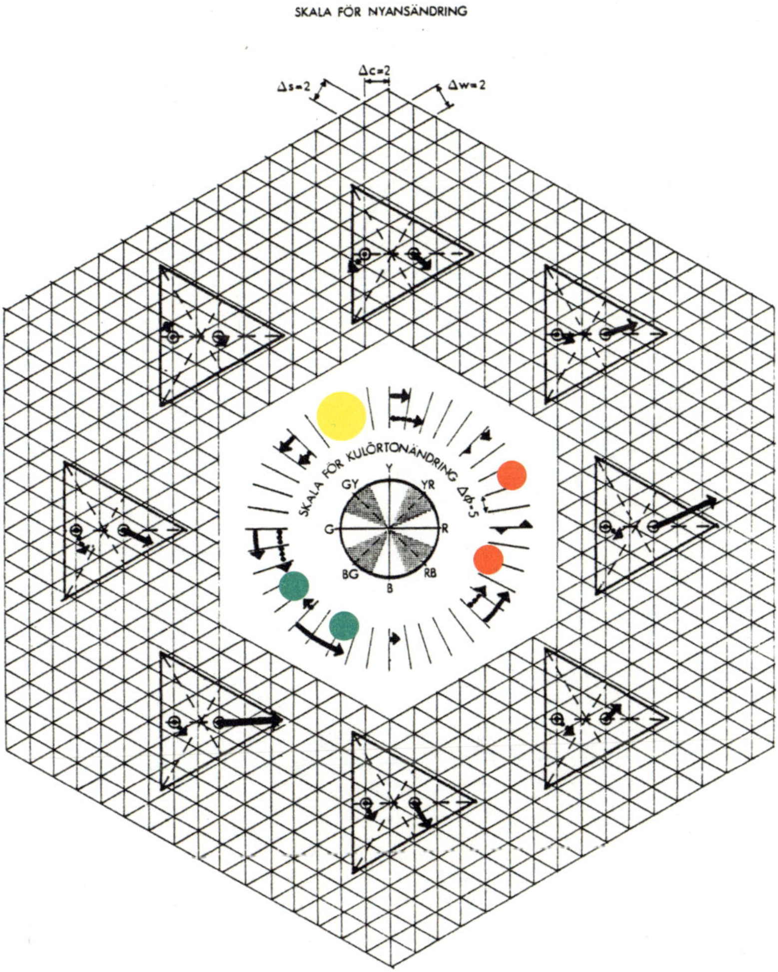

FIGURE 8. COLOUR CHANGES FOR DIFFERENT COLOUR GROUPS WHILE CHANGING LIGHT SOURCE FROM THE REFERENCE LIGHT SOURCE (SIMULATED DAYLIGHT) TO INCANDESCENT LIGHT. (SVEDMYR 1995 P. 90). THE INNER CIRCLE REPRESENTS LESS CHROMATIC NUANCES <15, THE OUTER CIRCLE REPRESENTS MORE CHROMATIC NUANCES >20.
COLOURED DOTS ARE MY ADDITION. BIG YELLOW DOT INDICATE BREAKING POINTS IN THE GREENISH YELLOW AREA FOR BOTH NUANCES USED. RED DOTS INDICATE BREAKING POINTS IN THE RED AREA. GREEN DOTS POINT OUT BREAKING POINTS IN THE GREEN-BLUE AREA FOR THE LESS CHROMATIC NUANCE ONLY.

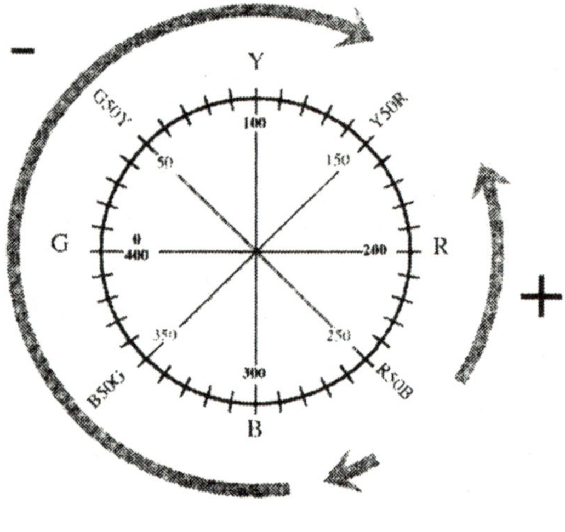

FIGURE 9. PRELIMINARY RESULTS BASED ON ASSESSMENTS OF 56 SAMPLES WITH INCANDESCENT LIGHT IN THE COLOUR REFERENCE BOX (BILLGER 1999 PAPER IV, P. 18).

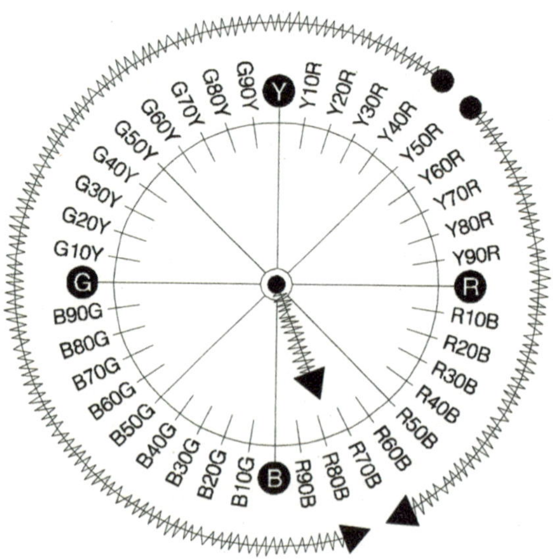

FIGURE 10. RECURRING TENDENCIES FOR HUE SHIFTS; FROM INHERENT TO PERCEIVED COLOUR. ARROWS INDICATE DIRECTIONS, NOT SIZES OF SHIFTS. (FRIDELL ANTER, 2000, P. 107)

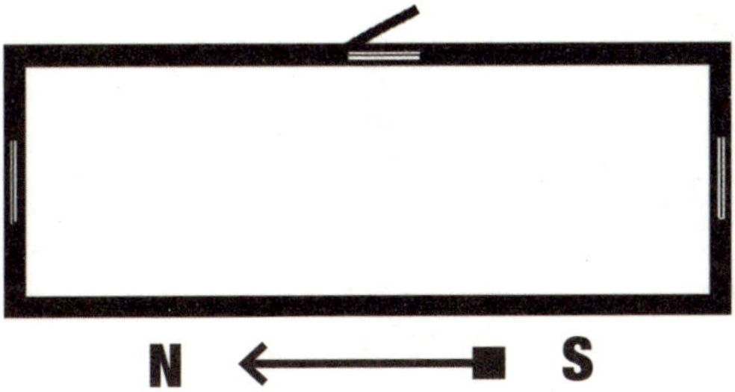

FIGURE 11. EXPERIMENT ROOM IN PHASE 1.

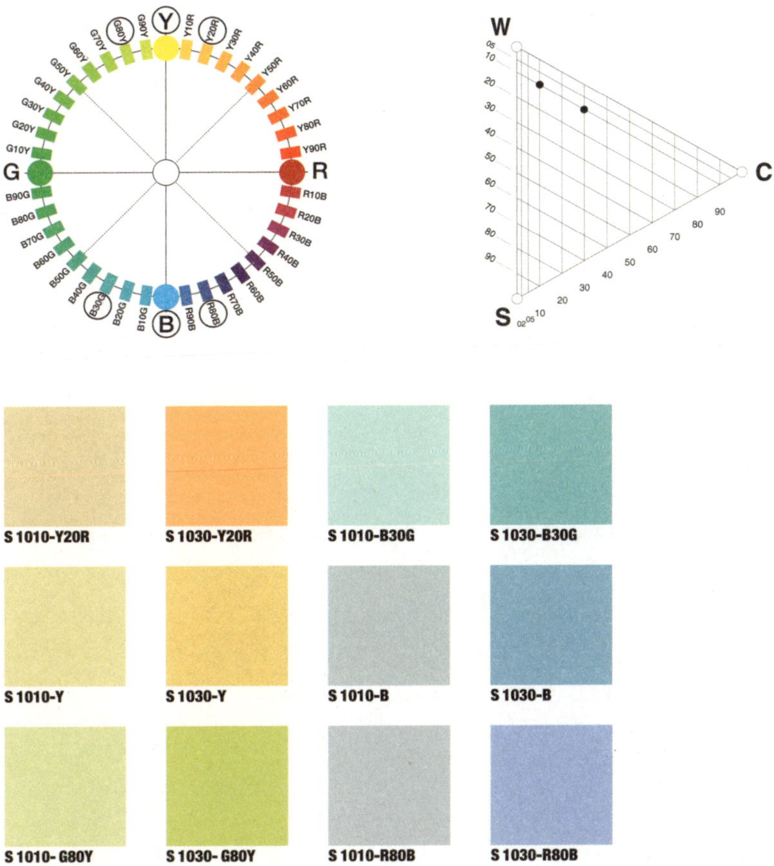

FIGURE 12. HUES AND NUANCES IN PHASE 1.

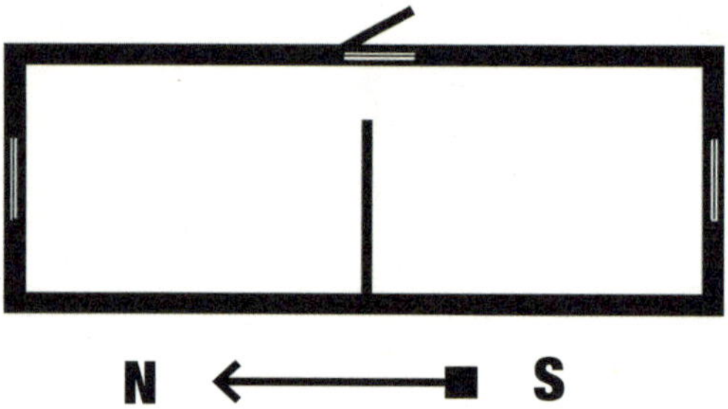

FIGURE 13. EXPERIMENT ROOMS IN PHASE 2.

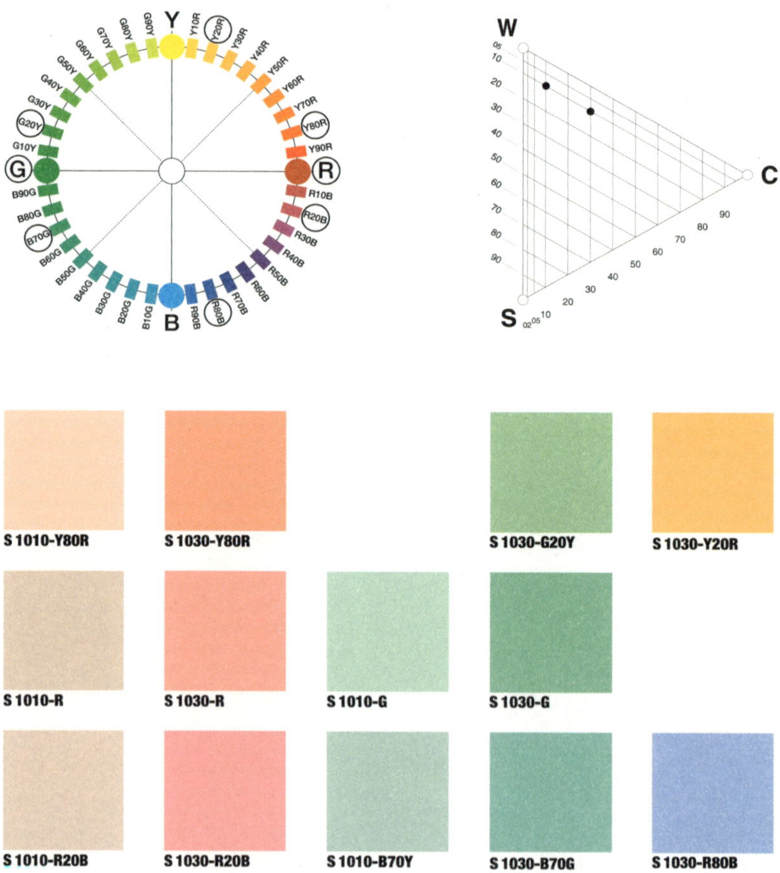

FIGURE 14. HUES AND NUANCES IN PHASE 2.

FIGURE 1. SUNLIGHT AND SKYLIGHT. PHOTO: BJÖRNER TORSSON.

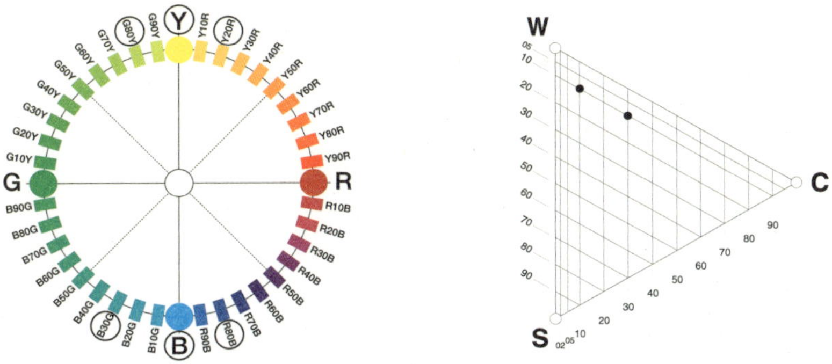

FIGURE 2. INHERENT COLOURS

FIGURE 3. ASSESSING COLOURS WITH THE COLOUR REFERENCE BOX

Identity colours
North

South

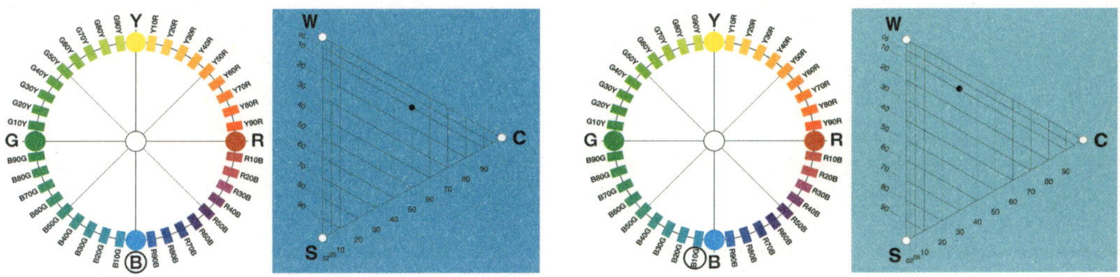

Colour Variations
North

South

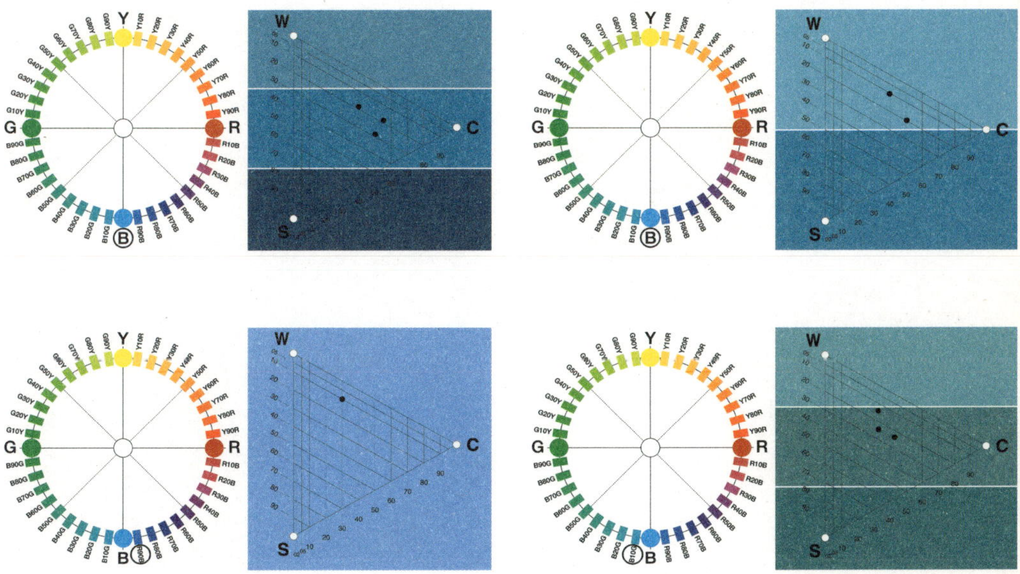

FIGURE 4. SHIFTS IN HUE AND NUANCE BETWEEN NORTH- AND SOUTH FACING ROOMS.
SHIFTS IN HUE AND NUANCE BETWEEN NORTH- AND SOUTH FACING ROOMS DUE TO THEIR COMPASS ORIENTATION. THE INHERENT COLOUR IS NCS S1030-B. FIGURES ABOVE THE LINE SHOW THE IDENTITY COLOUR IN THE NORTH- RESPECTIVELY SOUTH FACING ROOM, NORTH TO THE LEFT AND SOUTH TO THE WRIGHT. FIGURES UNDERNEATH THE LINE SHOW THE COLOUR VARIATIONS IN THE SAME STUDIES, BOTH HUE AND NUANCES. ALL TOGETHER, THESE FIGURES SHOW HOW THE DIFFERENCE IN COLOUR APPEARANCE BETWEEN TWO STUDIES RISES IN A GENERAL IMPRESSION.

Identity colours

North

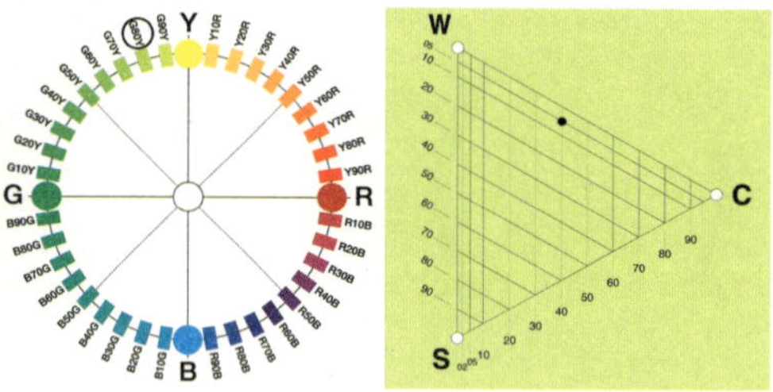

South

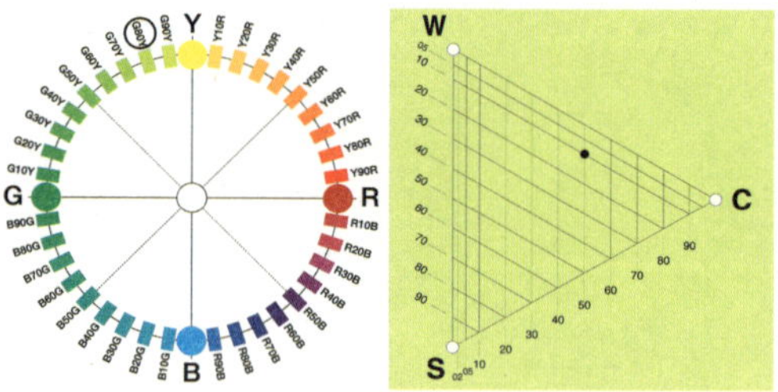

Colour Variations

North

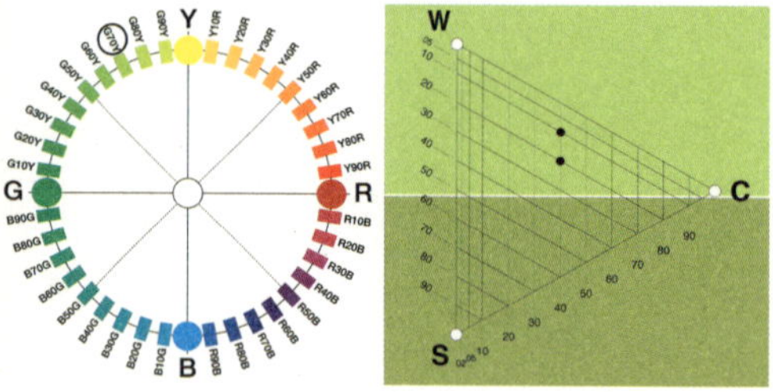

South

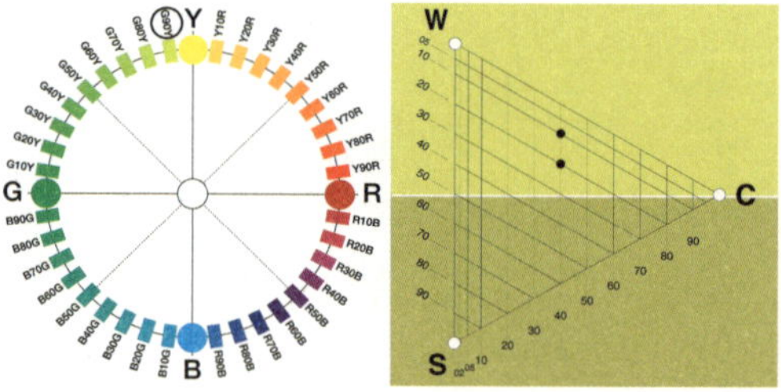

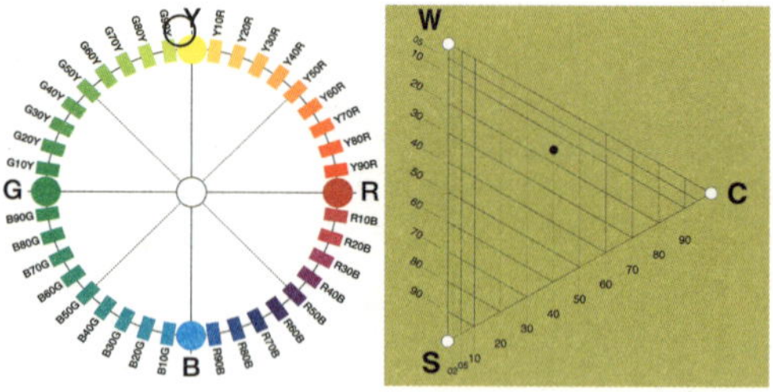

FIGURE 5. COLOUR VARIATIONS OFTEN WERE DECISIVE FOR COLOUR APPEARANCE
A GENERAL IMPRESSION OF A COLOUR SHIFT COULD ARISE FROM COLOUR VARIATIONS EVEN WHEN IT DID NOT SHOW IN THE IDENTITY COLOUR. IN THIS EXAMPLE THE INHERENT COLOUR IS NCS S 1030-G80Y.

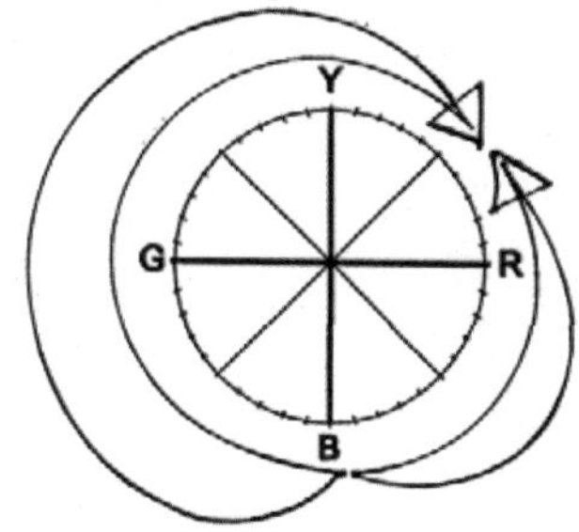

FIGURE 1: IN THE ARTIFICIAL LIGHT STUDY THE ADAPTATION EFFECT TENDED IN TWO DIRECTIONS FROM BETWEEN R90 AND B TOWARDS YELLOW-ORANGE

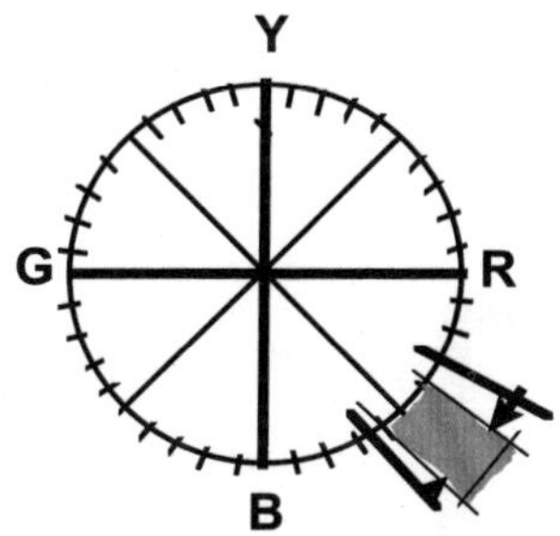

FIGUR 2. THE DIFFERENCE IS ADJUSTED 15 NCS-STEPS. AS A R30B-SAMPLE IS PERCEIVED AS APPROX. 10 STEPS MORE BLU-ISH IN THE COLOUR REFERENCE BOX THAN ITS PRINTED NCS-CODE, THE IDENTITY COLOUR IS 10 STEPS MORE BLUISH THAN THE NCS-CODE OF THE SAMPLE: I.E. R40B. AS A R65B-SAMPLE IS PER-CEIVED APPROX. 5 STEPS MORE REDDISH THAN ITS NCS-CODE, THE IDENTITY COLOUR IS 5 STEPS MORE REDDISH: I.E. R60B.

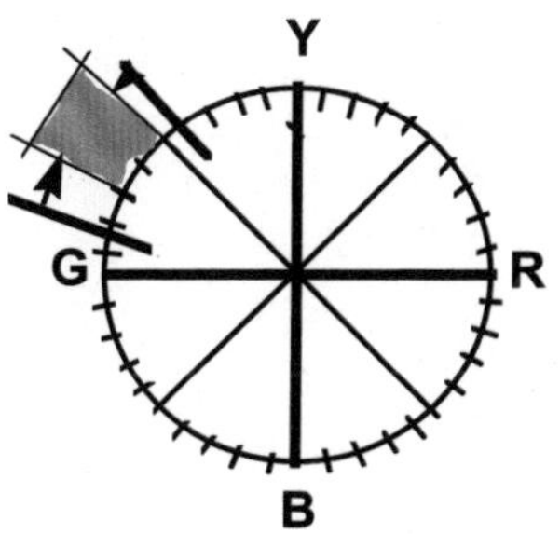

FIGUR 3. THE DIFFERENCE IS ADJUSTED 25 NCS-STEPS. AS A G60Y-SAMPLE IS PERCEIVED AS APPROX. 10 STEPS MORE GREENISH IN THE COLOUR REFERENCE BOX THAN ITS NCS-CODE, THE IDENTITY COLOUR OF THE WALL IS 10 STEPS MORE GREENISH: I.E. G50Y. AS A SAMPLE OF G15Y IS PERCEIVED AS APPROX. 15 STEPS MORE YELLOWISH IN THE COLOUR REFERENCE BOX THAN ITS NCS-CODE, THE IDENTITY COLOUR IS 15 STEPS MORE YELLOW-ISH: I.E. G30Y.

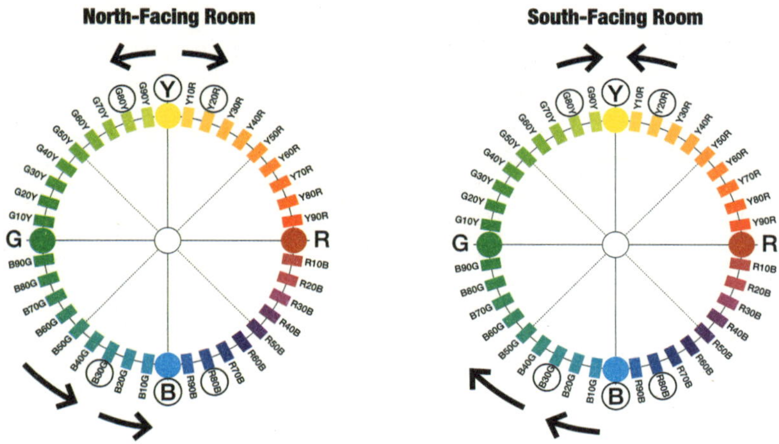

FIGURE 1. HUE SHIFT IN THE YELLOW-BLUE STUDY.
THE HUES SHIFT FROM ELEMENTARY YELLOW IN THE NORTH-FACING ROOM AND TOWARDS THE SAME IN THE SOUTH- FACING.

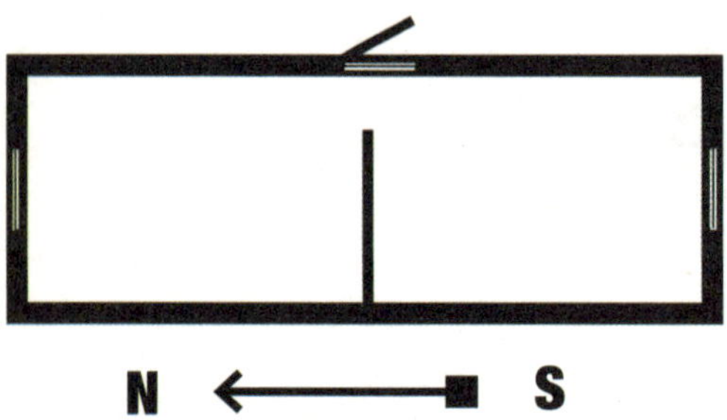

FIGURE 2. EXPERIMENTAL ROOMS
TWO EXPERIMENTAL ROOMS WERE SITUATED I
BUILDING SHED, PLACED IN A NORTH – SOUTH
DIRECTION. THE ROOMS MEASURED 4.20 X 2.9
OBSERVERS WERE SITTING SO AS TO OBSERVE
ROOM AT A TIME.

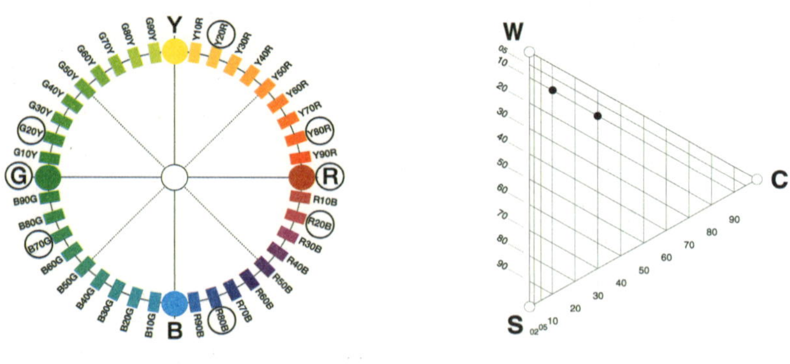

FIGURE 3. SELECTED COLOURS IN THE RED-GREEN STUDY.
THE NCS COLOUR CIRCLE SHOW THE EIGHT HUES CHOSEN AND THE NUANCE TRIANGLE SHOW THE NUANCES (WHITENESS, BLACKNESS AND CHROMATICNESS). THE INHERENT COLOURS AS FOLLOWS: EIGHT HUES AND TWO NUANCES (FIVE GREENISH AND SIX PINKISH COLOURS).
ONE YELLOWISH AND ONE BLUISH COLOUR IN ONE NUANCE ARE ADDED FOR REFERENCE PURPOSE.

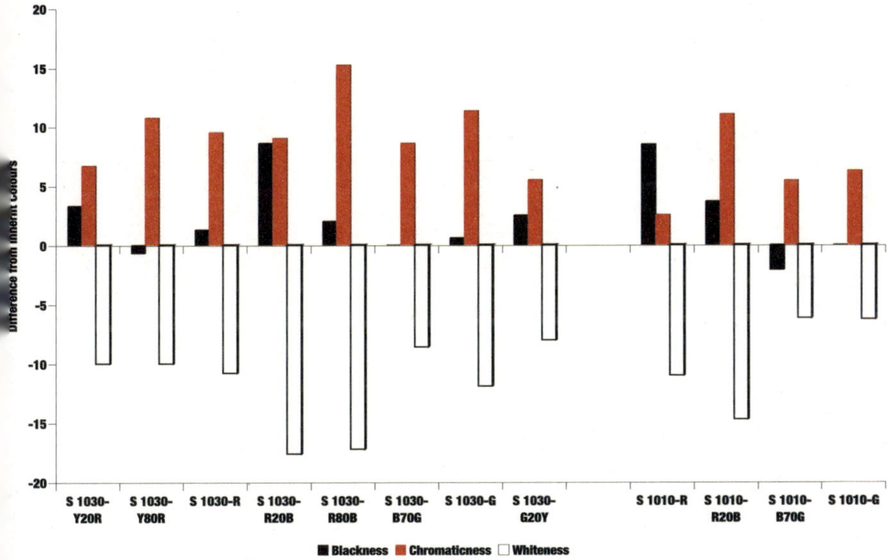

FIGURE 4. NUANCE SHIFT IN THE NORTH-FACING ROOM.
THE INHERENT COLOURS ARE REPRESENTED BY LEVEL ZERO; NUANCE 1030 HAS GREATER NUANCE SHIFT THAN 1010. BLUISH, REDDISH, AND GREENISH COLOURS INCREASE THE MOST IN CHROMATICNESS.

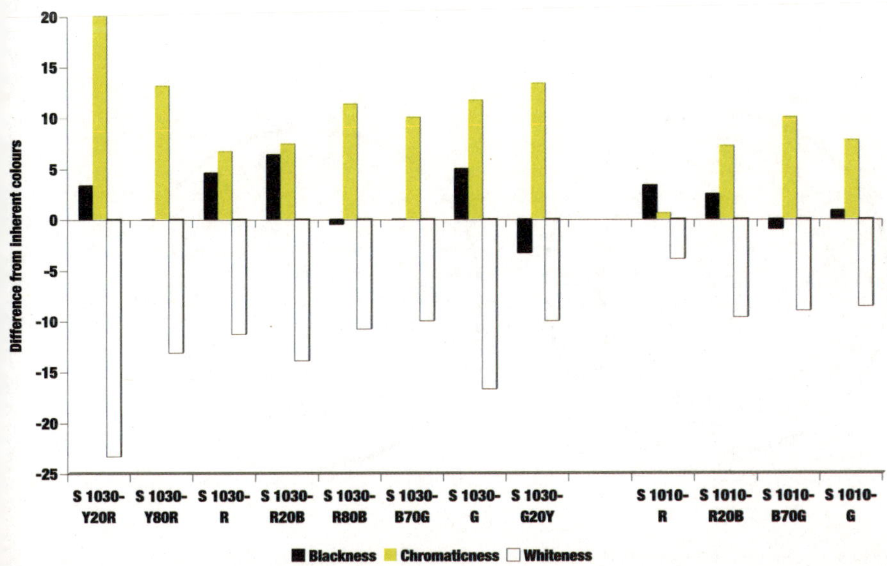

FIGURE 5. NUANCE SHIFT IN THE SOUTH-FACING ROOM.
THE INHERENT COLOURS ARE REPRESENTED BY LEVEL ZERO; NUANCE 1030 HAS GREATER NUANCE SHIFT THAN NUANCE 1010. YELLOW INCREASE THE MOST AND REDDISH THE LEAST IN CHROMATICNESS.

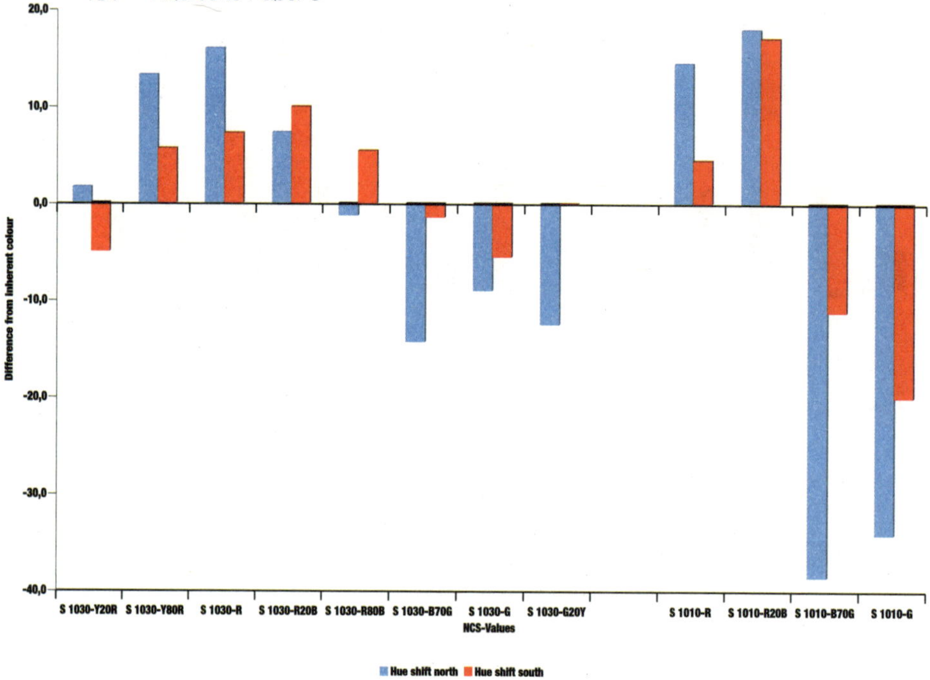

FIGURE 6. HUE SHIFT TENDENCIES IN COMPARISON BETWEEN THE ROOMS.
NUANCE 1010 HAS GREATER HUE SHIFT THAN 1030

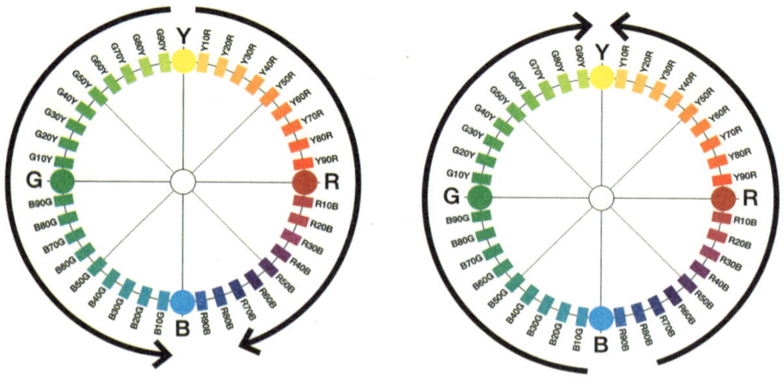

FIGURE 7. HUE SHIFT TENDENCIES IN BOTH ROOMS.
RESULTS COMPILED FROM THE YELLOW-BLUE AND THE RED- GREEN STUDIES; THE TWO COMPASS ORIENTATIONS INVOLVED CAUSED OPPOSING HUE SHIFT TENDENCIES; THE COLOURS TENDED TO BE MORE BLUISH IN THE NORTH-FACING AND MORE YELLOWISH IN THE SOUTH-FACING ROOM

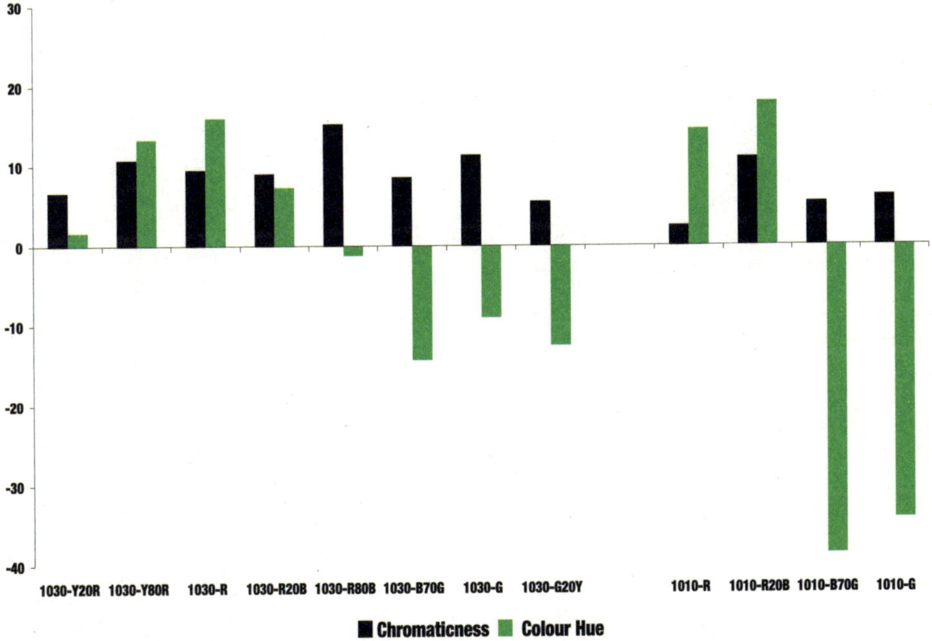

FIGURE 8. COLOUR SHIFTS IN THE NORTH-FACING ROOM.
THE HUE SHIFT TENDENCY INCREASED MOST IN THIS ROOM, CHANGING FROM YELLOWISH TOWARDS ELEMENTARY BLUE. THE GREATEST CHROMATIC INCREASE WAS FOUND IN THE BLUISH, REDDISH AND GREENISH COLOURS.

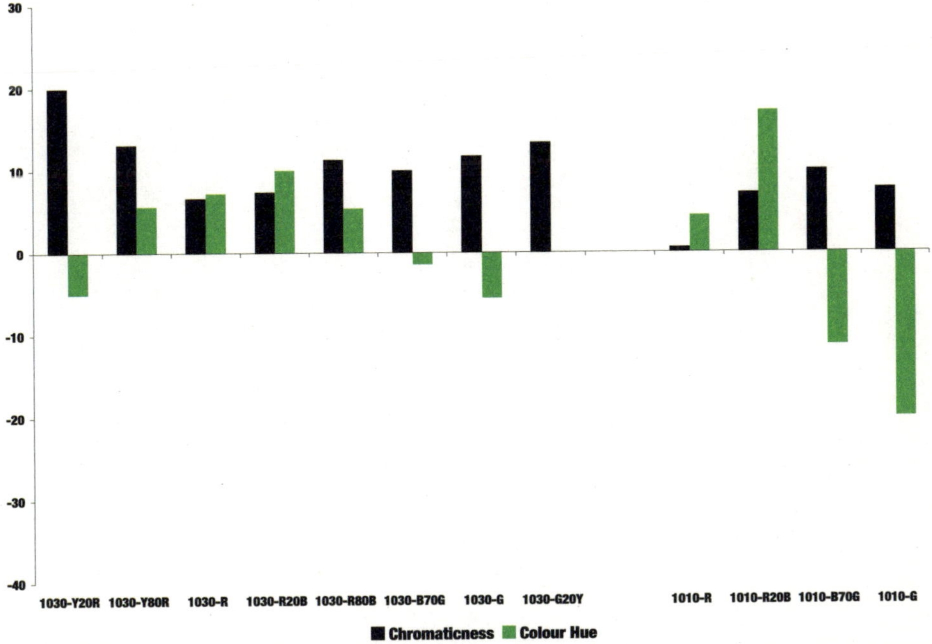

FIGURE 9. COLOUR SHIFTS IN THE SOUTH-FACING ROOM.
THE CHROMATICNESS INCREASED MOST IN THIS ROOM WITH YELLOWISH AND GREENISH COLOURS SHOWING THE GREATEST CHROMATIC INCREASE. THE HUE SHIFT TENDENCY WENT TOWARDS INCREASED YELLOWNESS

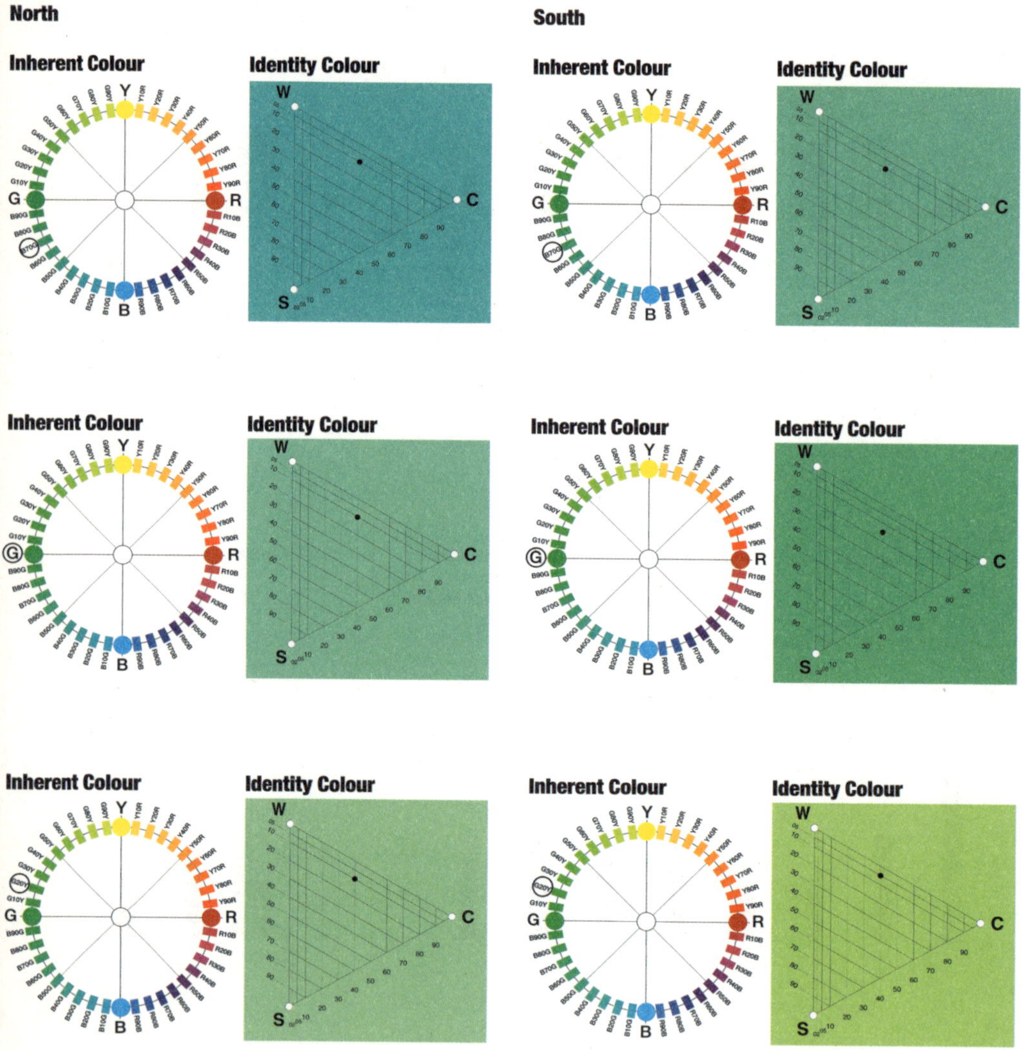

JRE 10. GREENISH COLOURS IN BOTH ROOMS.
.OUR APPEARANCES FROM THE NORTH-FACING ROOM ARE DISPLAYED TO THE LEFT AND THE SOUTH-FACING TO THE RIGHT; TOP)30-B70G, MIDDLE S1030-G, BOTTOM S 1030-G20Y. INHERENT COLOUR SHOWN IN COLOUR CIRCLE, IDENTITY COLOUR SHOWN IN .OUR TRIANGLE AS NUANCE AND BACKGROUND COLOUR.

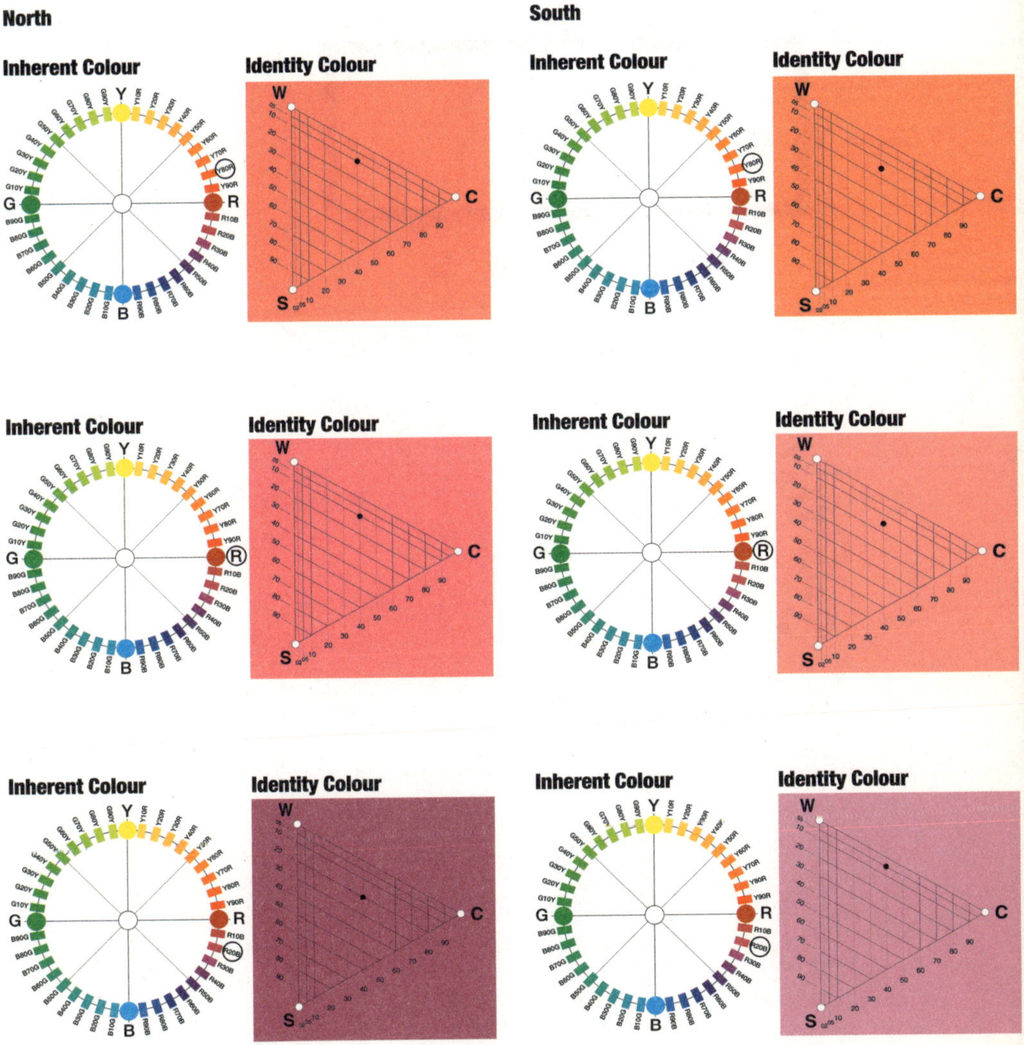

FIGURE 11. PINKISH COLOURS IN BOTH ROOMS.
TOP S 1030-Y80R, MIDDLE S 1030-R, BOTTOM S 1030-R20B. INHERENT COLOUR SHOWN IN COLOUR CIRCLE, IDENTITY COLOUR SHOWN IN COLOUR TRIANGLE AS NUANCE AND BACKGROUND COLOUR.

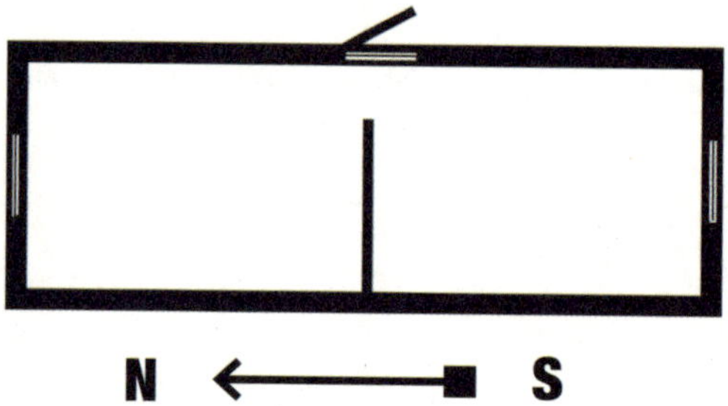

FIGURE 1. EXPERIMENTAL ROOMS.
TWO SIMILAR FULL-SCALE ROOMS WERE SET UP IN A CONSTRUCTION CABIN POSITIONED FACING NORTH – SOUTH, MEASURING 4.2 M X 2.9 M EACH. BOTH ROOMS HAD SIMILAR SHORT-END WINDOWS.

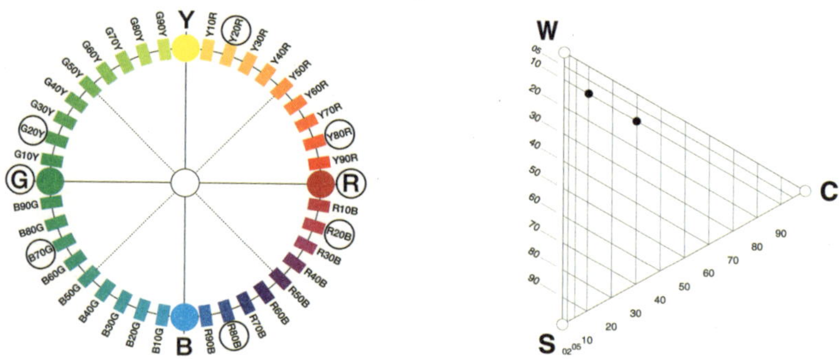

FIGURE 2. SELECTED HUES AND NUANCES.
THREE HUES IN TWO NUANCES, IN TOTAL SIX PINKISH AND FIVE GREENISH COLOURS.

FIGURE 3. COLOUR DISPLAY.

S 1030-B70G	S 1030-G	S 1030-G20Y	
DIGNIFIED RESTRAINED	ALIVE VERSUS PLASTIC DISGUSTING VERSUS RESTFUL	DISSOCIATION ARTIFICIAL	**NORTH**
CALM COOL FRESH PURE INTENSE	FRESH CLEAN TRANQUIL SLOW	CALM UNSOPHISTICATED CLUMSY SAD	**REPETETIVE DESCRIPTION FOR ROOMS IN BOTH COMPASS ORIENTATIONS**
WARM EMPTY	WARM CALM EMBRACING SOOTHING	WARM	**SOUTH**

FIGURE 4. DIFFERENCES IN VERBAL DESCRIPTIONS
MOST FREQUENTLY USED VERBAL DESCRIPTIONS WHEN EVALUATING PINKISH ROOMS IN THE NORTH- RESPECTIVELY SOUTH COMPASS DIRECTION. THE MIDDLE SECTION SHOWS DESCRIPTIONS IN COMMON FOR THE TWO.

	S 1030-Y80R	S 1030-R	S 1030-R20B
NORTH	INTENSE DARKER COLDER	COLD ALIVE ADULT	DIGNIFIED RESTRAINED
REPETETIVE DESCRIPTION FOR ROOMS IN BOTH COMPASS ORIENTATIONS	SNUG SECURE EMBRACING PUSHY DOMINANT	SOFT PUSHY IMPORTUNATE TRYING	NOSTALGIC STRONG INDEPENDENT UN-FRESH
SOUTH	SOFT FLUFFY ENERGETIC ALIVE	WARM YOUNG RELAXING	BRAVE CHEERFUL FUNNY ROMANTIC

FIGURE 5. DIFFERENCES IN VERBAL DESCRIPTIONS.
MOST FREQUENTLY USED VERBAL DESCRIPTIONS WHEN EVALUATING GREENISH ROOMS IN THE NORTH- RESPECTIVELY SOUTH COMPASS DIRECTION. THE MIDDLE SECTION SHOWS DESCRIPTIONS IN COMMON FOR THE TWO.

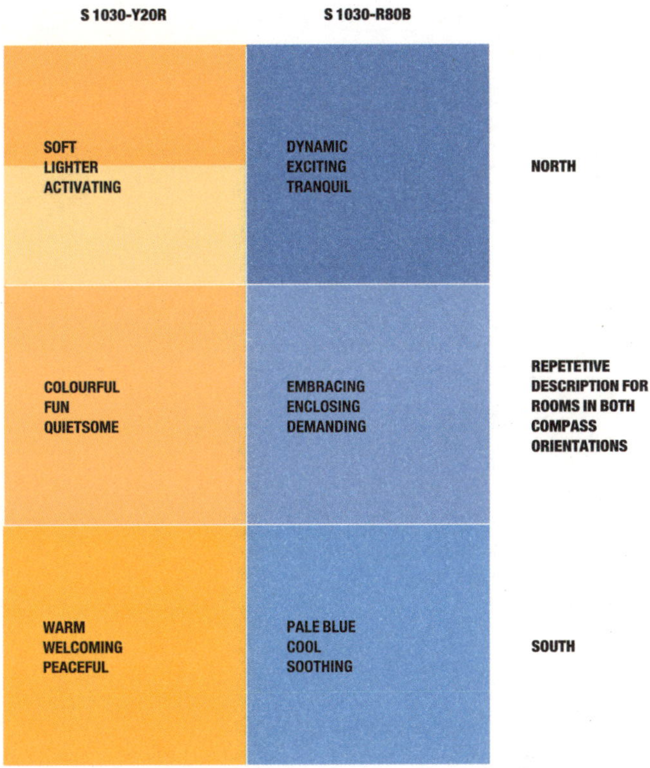

FIGURE 6. DIFFERENCES IN VERBAL DESCRIPTIONS.
MOST FREQUENTLY USED VERBAL DESCRIPTIONS WHEN EVALUATING GREENISH ROOMS IN THE NORTH- RESPECTIVELY SOUTH COMPASS DIRECTION. THE MIDDLE SECTION SHOWS DESCRIPTIONS IN COMMON FOR THE TWO.

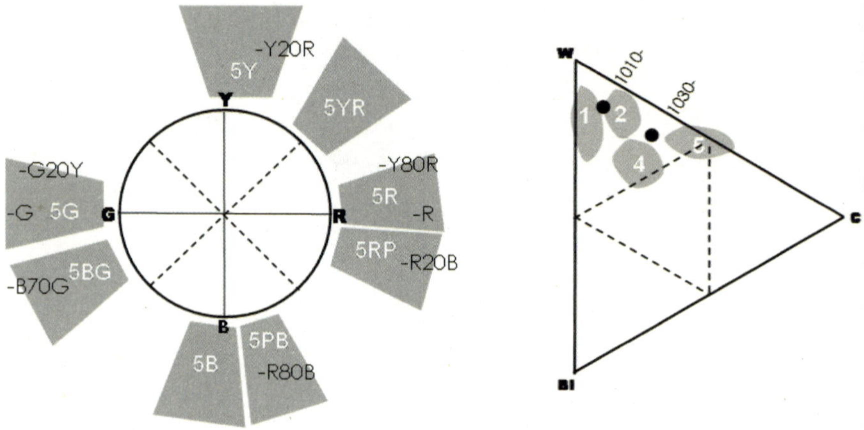

FIGURE 1. LEFT: THE GREY AREAS WITH WHITE TEXT ARE THE HUE AREAS IN CE. THE BLACK TEXT SHOWS THE HUES OF THE ROOM STUDY. RIGHT: NUANCE AREAS IN CE WITH WHITE TEXT. BLACK TEXT AND MARK FOR THE ROOM STUDY.